Mastering Alternative Dispute Resolution

Mastering Evidence
Ronald W. Eades

Mastering Family Law
Janet Leach Richards

Mastering Income Tax
Christopher M. Pietruszkiewicz, Gail Levin Richmond

Mastering Intellectual Property
George W. Kuney, Donna C. Looper

Mastering Labor Law
Paul M. Secunda, Anne Marie Lofaso, Joseph E. Slater, Jeffrey M. Hirsch

Mastering Legal Analysis and Communication
David T. Ritchie

Mastering Legal Analysis and Drafting
George W. Kuney, Donna C. Looper

Mastering Negotiable Instruments (UCC Articles 3 and 4)
and Other Payment Systems
Michael D. Floyd

Mastering Partnership Taxation
Stuart Lazar

Mastering Products Liability
Ronald W. Eades

Mastering Professional Responsibility, 2d e
Grace M. Giesel

Mastering Property Law
Darryl C. Wilson, Cynthia H. DeBose

Mastering Secured Transactions (UCC Article 9) 2d e
Richard H. Nowka

Mastering Statutory Interpretation 2d e
Linda D. Jellum

Mastering Tort Law
Russell L. Weaver, Edward C. Martin, Andrew R. Klein,
Paul J. Zwier II, Ronald W. Eades, John H. Bauman

Mastering Trademark and Unfair Competition Law
Lars S. Smith, Llewellyn Joseph Gibbons

Mastering Alternative Dispute Resolution

Kelly M. Feeley

PROFESSOR OF LAW
STETSON UNIVERSITY COLLEGE OF LAW

James A. Sheehan

PROFESSOR OF LAW
STETSON UNIVERSITY COLLEGE OF LAW

CAROLINA ACADEMIC PRESS
Durham, North Carolina

Library of Congress Cataloging in Publication Data

Library of Congress Cataloging-in-Publication Data

Feeley, Kelly M., author.
 Mastering alternative dispute resolution / Kelly M. Feeley and James
A. Sheehan.
    pages cm. -- (Carolina Academic Press Mastering Series)
 Includes bibliographical references and index.
 ISBN 978-1-61163-201-9 (alk. paper)
 1. Dispute resolution (Law)--United States. I. Sheehan, James,
1949- author. II. Title.

 KF9084.F44 2014
 347.73'9--dc23

                              2014035890

Carolina Academic Press
700 Kent Street
Durham, NC 27701
Telephone (919) 489-7486
Fax (919) 493-5668
www.cap-press.com

To Patty Ann

No one fought harder, smiled wider, or loved deeper. I love you, miss you and am inspired by you every day! You are truly my sister, my friend, and my hero.

Contents

Series Editor's Foreword

The Carolina Academic Press Mastering Series is designed to provide you with a tool that will enable you to easily and efficiently "master" the substance and content of law school courses. Throughout the series, the focus is on quality writing that makes legal concepts understandable. As a result, the series is designed to be easy to read and is not unduly cluttered with footnotes or cites to secondary sources.

In order to facilitate student mastery of topics, the Mastering Series includes a number of pedagogical features designed to improve learning and retention. At the beginning of each chapter, you will find a "Roadmap" that tells you about the chapter and provides you with a sense of the material that you will cover. A "Checkpoint" at the end of each chapter encourages you to stop and review the key concepts, reiterating what you have learned. Throughout the book, key terms are explained and emphasized. Finally, a "Master Checklist" at the end of each book reinforces what you have learned and helps you identify any areas that need review or further study.

We hope that you will enjoy studying with, and learning from, the Mastering Series.

Russell L. Weaver
Professor of Law & Distinguished University Scholar
University of Louisville, Louis D. Brandeis School of Law

Introduction

This is a book about negotiation, mediation, and arbitration. It's a handbook, an introduction to these three skills. You won't find a whole lot of footnotes in this book or case citations. Negotiation, mediation, and arbitration are skills. They are taught differently than most other law school subjects. They are usually taught by doing, although there are some fundamentals that need to be learned. This book will discuss the fundamentals and use examples to show how to put those fundamentals to practical use. It is designed to get you started on your understanding of these particular fields of endeavor. We, the authors of this book, were practicing attorneys before we were professors, and the skills we are going to discuss come primarily, but not exclusively, from our actual experience. Just as 100 people can look at the same piece of artwork and have 100 different perspectives and reactions, there are many theories about how negotiations, mediations, and arbitrations are to be conducted. We couldn't and are not going to cover every theory or every possibility. This book will give you a general overview of the three subjects, which will give you some basic tools, and from there you can develop your own style of doing things through your experience and your own research. Think of this book as helping to stock your legal tool belt, along with the knowledge to know when and how to use a particular tool.

With these initial thoughts in mind, let's begin.

Mastering Alternative
Dispute Resolution

Chapter 1

The ADR Process

So why negotiation, mediation, and arbitration? They represent what is commonly known as alternative dispute resolution (ADR) or, more simply, ways to resolve disputes without going to trial. Many variations of each of these ADR methods have actually been in existence since people began dealing with each other. So are we really saying that for hundreds of years, people have been negotiating? Yes, even if not in a formal sit-down fashion. And what about mediation? Yes again, as people have asked a third party to hear each side's story and then have the third party weigh in. But arbitration is pretty new, right? Not exactly, because as early as 1768, the New York Chamber of Commerce was using arbitration to resolve disputes.[1] However, even though negotiation, mediation, and arbitration have been around in some form or another for hundreds of years, during the past 50 years,[2] they have become much more prevalent in the legal system as recognized ways to effectively resolve disputes. It is from this perspective that we review each process in the legal context to help you better understand how and when to engage in one or more of these processes, and how to do so more effectively.

We also approach each process with the understanding that many things happen before an attorney would engage in any of them. Interviewing and getting to know your client would be the first and most important step before representing that client. That would also involve investigating the client's claims, which takes some time. An attorney must gather evidence, secure witnesses, observe and photograph the scene, review documents, and of course conduct research. It's been said that a client's case never sounds so good as it does on the first day the client tells it. That's accurate because usually you don't get the full story on day one. Understandably, clients want to highlight the positive aspects of their case and downplay or omit any negatives. Sometimes that is done intentionally, and other times, it's just human nature. People don't relish the thought of pointing out their faults; however, a lawyer's job is to discover and

---

1. Jay Folberg, Dwight Gloann, Lisa Loppenberg, and Thomas Stipanowich *Resolving Disputes: Theory, Practice and Law*, 455 (Aspen 2005).
2. Id. at 5.

process all relevant information so that the lawyer can best represent that client. Interviewing, counseling, and investigating would require another book altogether, but it is important to understand the role they play in legal representation. No matter how successful negotiation, mediation, or arbitration can be, they will not be if lawyers are not fully informed about their client's case and are not fully prepared to address the case from all angles.

Chapter 2

Negotiation

Roadmap

- There are many essential Negotiation Tools for an advocate to master, including the ability to:
  - Communicate
  - Listen
  - Understand
  - Empathize
  - Choose the Right Words
  - Step into Someone Else's Shoes
  - Deal Directly with Emotional Issues
- The process of Negotiation can be broken down into some discrete categories:
  - Preparation
  - Strategy
  - Timing
  - Patience
  - Fact Finding
  - Identifying Mutual Interests
  - Flexibility
  - Reasons
  - Movement
  - Creative Solutions
  - Openness

Learning how to effectively negotiate is an essential skill for an advocate. Some might say it is an essential skill for everyone on the planet who breathes, but that's a subject for another day. As we stated in the introduction, we don't teach skills courses the same way we teach academic courses. You can't get the skill by listening to a lecture. You can only learn by doing. How then do you write a book about negotiation? Good question. With any skill, you need to have some understanding of the basics of the process. It is similar to learning chemistry. You wouldn't just go into the lab and start mixing chemicals together and wait to see what happens, and if you did, you might cause a fire or an explosion. Instead, you would take a chemistry class first to understand chemical compounds, bonds, and reactions. Then with the basic understanding of chemistry, you would be led through lab experiments, and ultimately, allowed to work on your own. The same is true of legal skills, including negotiation. As stated previously, there are many correct and effective approaches to negotiation, but most start with some key principles or basics. So to do that, we are going to try something different, at least in this part of the book that deals with negotiation. We are going to talk about the skills and try and learn the skills through real life situations or, more accurately, real life situations made up by the authors.

I. Communication and Emotions

Pete and Gladys have been married for five years and they have two children, Peter Jr., age 3, and Johnny, age 1. Pete is an air conditioner mechanic and Gladys is a stay-at-home mom who does side work for a time-share company, cold-calling prospective customers when she has spare time. Pete is constantly worried about making enough money to support the family. He's working six days a week, sometimes ten hours a day. He never turns down work and he is always tired. Gladys, on the other hand, has her hands full with two boys full of energy and vigor who never stop going. Gladys also runs the house and, in her spare time, sells time shares.

One day, Gladys has had enough and just explodes at Pete.

"You're never around and when you are all you do is sleep. I get no help from you. I get no support. I get no love."

Pete hears Gladys' words and explodes back: "You have no idea what I do. How hard I work for this family. You're so self-centered. I don't even know why I stay here."

"I don't know why you do either." Gladys replies. And so it begins.

Pete doesn't leave but he's angry and he's hurt, and he retreats to his corner when he comes home and watches television. Gladys has her own corner. It could be the kitchen washing dishes or the laundry room doing laundry, or the bedroom where she talks to her mother on the phone.

About now you might be thinking you picked up the wrong book. This is obviously a book about counseling. It could be, but it's not. It's a book about negotiation. *Why*, you might ask, *are you talking about a domestic quarrel in a book about negotiation?*

This is the best place to start because negotiation at its core is communication or, very commonly, miscommunication. What is communication? Is it just talking to each other? Pete and Gladys are talking to each other but are they really communicating? Is Gladys telling Pete how she really feels or is she just lashing out at him *because* of how she feels? Is Pete really hearing her or is he just getting defensive and lashing back at her? Obviously the answer is that Gladys is lashing out and so is Pete and there is very little communication going on, even though they were at one time talking to each other. Pete doesn't really hear Gladys' pain and he certainly doesn't feel it. He immediately gets defensive and starts formulating his reply—his defense. Gladys does the same.

What if Gladys, instead of lashing out at Pete, said something like, "Pete, I'm so tired. I'm just running on empty. I don't know what to do. I know you're busy too but I need help. I need a break."

Pete might not be listening and he might get defensive anyway, but if Pete did take the time to really hear his wife—to put himself in her shoes—he would start to understand. *She's home all day with these kids. She never gets out. It's not a glamorous job cooking, cleaning, doing everybody's dirty, smelly laundry. She probably is at her wits' end.*

And what if Pete said to Gladys, "I'm sorry, honey. I know things are piling up on you and I wish I was there more often. And I know even when I'm home, I'm not there, because I'm just too tired. I'm working too much but if I stop, I'm worried that we won't have enough money to survive"? Would Gladys tell him to go blow it out his ear? I don't think so.

Communication is not just about talking to each other. Communication is about searching for the right words to express how you feel. Taking the extra time to really think about what you are going to say *and* how it might be received. If Gladys had taken any time to think about what reaction Pete would have to her words, she probably would not have said what she did. *Doesn't everybody say things they shouldn't say when they are emotional*, you ask? Not everybody. If you stop and think about your words before you say them, you can reverse the silly merry-go-round of lashing out and reacting because it is not effective communication.

But don't stop there. Speaking is only one side of the art of communication. The other side is listening. Let me say that again: the other side is listening! Yes, Pete has his own grievances. Yes, Pete is exhausted from all the hours he is working. But that does not take away from Gladys' feelings. It doesn't make her any less tired. Pete needs to hear her and validate her, and then at the appropriate time when he thinks they will be received well, he can communicate his feelings.

Listening wouldn't do any good, *you might say,* because Gladys didn't communicate her feelings. She just lashed out at Pete. [*What did she say?*] *"You're never around and when you are, all you do is sleep. I get no help from you. I get no support. I get no love."* Pete lives in that house. He knows what Gladys does. He knows she has to be exhausted. Is it that much of a leap for him to stop and think about her words and think about what's really going on and then validate her feelings?

What if Pete did that and said to his wife — "I know that you are tired, honey. I know what you do around here. I do. And I know that I'm not around as much as I should be." Would he not have gone a long way towards dissipating Gladys' anger?

Let's get out of the domestic realm and bring this discussion of communication into the commercial context. There may be a difference in tone and subject matter but I suggest to you the same issues are at work. People are the same whether at home or at work. Corporations are run by people and people are emotional beings.

George Deely contracts with A and E Moving Company to move his furniture from his old house to his new house. As part of its services, A and E offers insurance to cover any damage to the furniture occasioned by the move. George is told that the insurance would eliminate any arguments over who was at fault for the move, so he decides to take the insurance. There is a $1,000 deductible. During the move, several pieces of valuable furniture are damaged including a painting valued from $30,000 to $60,000 depending on who you talk to. George files a claim with the insurance company for $80,000, complies with all the requests for documentation, and ultimately receives a settlement offer of $125. George also learns that there is no insurance company. The so-called insurance company is actually A and E Moving Company. George is livid. He contacts his attorney and tells him he wants to sue. The attorney sends a demand letter, which is a letter that states why A and E is responsible for what happened, describes George's damages, and requests or demands an amount to resolve the matter.

Meanwhile, there is a change of leadership at A and E Moving Company. The new CEO, Art, is a more modern manager. He plans on bringing the company into the twenty-first century by computerizing everything and changing the marketing strategy, which is from the Dark Ages. The first problem he runs into is the George Deely situation. When he researches the problem, he realizes that the whole insurance premium business is a scam. The premium is paid to the company, but the company never pays a claim. Why? Because the company requires the deductible be paid up front before it will even process a claim and the customer is not willing to pay the deductible up front. The Deely claim is substantial, however, and it's pretty clear George Deely is not going to just go away. Art also knows that Deely could get punitive damages[1] if he uncovers the company's fraudulent scheme. Punitive damages could ruin the company financially. Art decides he needs to do something quickly so he calls his lawyer, Paul, and tells him to set up a meeting with Deely's lawyer.

Before the meeting with Deely and his lawyer, Art meets with Paul to discuss strategy.

"I know what you're afraid of," Paul tells him after Art explains the situation. "But I think we need to go in there with the attitude that we're ready to go to court. That we stand by our policy but that we're ready to listen. We can give a little but we need to be firm at the outset."

Art usually listens to his lawyer's advice. However, he also knows Paul is a litigator and as a litigator he has to play a certain role for his client—that of the warrior. "We have to stand firm. We can only give a little."

Art sees this one differently. He thinks of George Deely and how angry George must be at losing a piece of art and then being virtually slapped in the face with a settlement offer of $125. George was also probably pretty angry when he found out that he really didn't have insurance—that his insurance payment was just a little extra payment to A and E Moving Company. Art is not a lawyer but he has been dealing with people his entire life. He knows instinctively that playing tough under these circumstances is not going to work.

Who is right? Does Art's lawyer with all his litigation experience have the right approach? Should Art defer to his lawyer?

The longer you're in the legal field, the more firmly you become convinced that there is no right way or wrong way to do things. What works for one lawyer might not work for another. The best you can do when you are conducting an analysis like we are doing here is find the most reasonable approach that will work for most people most of the time.[2] Sometimes it's good to be strong and forceful and sometimes it isn't, and we will get into that discussion a little later on in this book. As for this particular problem in this particular case, let's see what works.

The meeting date arrives. Art wants to make the opening statement and tells his lawyer to follow his lead. His lawyer does not object to Art's strategy

---

1. Punitive damages are damages meant to punish the wrongdoer for egregious behavior to stop it from happening again. Because they are designed to punish or hurt, punitive damages are generally much higher than the actual value of the claim itself. It is not uncommon to see punitive damages reach 3 times or more than the amount of the claim.

2. We often tell our students that a lawyer's job is to offend the least amount of people the most amount of time!

but, as he must and you must in all cases, insists on knowing what his client is going to say before they walk into the meeting room.

The negotiation begins with the parties introducing themselves and exchanging pleasantries—and don't do this too quickly. A lot can be accomplished by making small talk before the negotiation begins. Maybe Art and George went to the same college or maybe they grew up in the same geographical area. There is usually something you can find in common.

"Do you know so and so?"

"I knew of him. He went to school with my older sister. Great athlete."

And so it begins. A connection is made. It's not going to solve the problem but it may dissipate the emotion. Maybe not. In any event, after the pleasantries are exchanged, Art starts the meeting.

"George, I've asked you and your counsel to be here today because I want to clear the air about certain things and I want to apologize to you personally for the way you have been treated by my company. First of all, we should have made it clear that we are not an insurance company, we are just acting like an insurance company the way a company that was self-insured would act. Second, we did not act like an insurance company in your particular case. If we did, we would have processed your claim and made you a reasonable offer. Third, the offer we made to you was an insult.

"I cannot erase what has happened in the past. I can only acknowledge the mistake, apologize, and hope we can move on from here. I am here to resolve this matter today if we can."

Now George is sitting on the other side of the table ready to burst. He heard the small talk between Art and the two lawyers, but he didn't participate at all. He didn't even want to come. He only did it because his lawyer insisted. Now, the president of this company is sitting directly across from him, looking him in the eye, and validating every feeling that he has. *Maybe this guy is serious. Maybe I'll just listen to what he has to say.*

Now you might be thinking Art has gone way too far. He basically fell on his sword. He's got nowhere to go. You might be wrong. Art has done his homework. He knows this claim is worth somewhere between $50,000 and $80,000, depending on which valuation of the painting that was destroyed you choose, and Art wants to get closer to the $50,000 figure than the $80,000 one. He also knows that his company could be looking at a punitive damage claim that far exceeds the $80,000 figure. But Art also knows he can never get to the discussion of what a reasonable amount is unless he can get George to listen and the only way to get George to listen is to validate his feelings and let him know, *even though he has not even spoken,* that you hear him or, as they say in my neighborhood, that you feel him.

On the other hand, let's say Art's lawyer, Paul, has convinced Art that his way is the best way. So Paul opens the conversation.

"We're happy to be here and we are hopeful we can get this resolved but there are some things we want you to know. We are a major company. We've been in business for twenty years. And our policies and procedures have been in place that long as well. We have a strong legal basis for what we do and we only make reasonable offers. Having said that, we are here to listen and if we hear additional information we may be willing to adjust our offer."

Whose opening makes more sense? Whose opening is more likely to begin the process of resolving the dispute? Obviously, Art's approach is the better approach in this situation, but I can assure you, after practicing law for more than thirty years, that Art's approach would very rarely be used.

We will follow Pete and Gladys and George and Art's stories in the pages that follow. For now, however, keep in mind this one thought: Most negotiations involve some emotional issues. If you address those issues in an honest and straightforward manner at the outset, your chances of having a successful negotiation improve substantially.

Stop Points

1. If there are emotional issues involved in a particular dispute, and you address them at the outset, your chances of reaching a resolution will be greatly increased.
2. To communicate effectively, you need to think about what you are going to say and how it is going to be received. Venting or *lashing out* will get you nowhere because you are not communicating your true feelings.
3. To communicate effectively, you need to *listen* to what is being said. Do not get defensive and try to formulate a response to justify your actions. Validate the message and the messenger.
4. Even when the message is not clear, try to see through it and understand what the other side is trying to say.

II. Preparation

You may be surprised to learn this or you may not have thought about it at all, but many lawyers go into a negotiation without preparing a lick. The thought process goes something like this: *I know my case. I know my client. I know where I want to start and I know where I want to end up. What else is there?* Those lawyers would be at a distinct disadvantage if they went into the negotiation room with you, a lawyer who is well prepared. What do you have to prepare for? The short answer is everything. The long answer is a little more complicated. It's what Professor Charlie Rose here at Stetson calls "the Necessary."

What is "the Necessary" in negotiation? More than anything, it is sitting down and analyzing what your interests are and how you are going to go about getting your interests met. And remember, interests are not just numbers or dollars, they are people's situations, motivations, needs, fears, etc.

Let's go back to Pete and Gladys to begin this discussion. And let's say they have decided to take a break, to separate for a period of time to see if they want to continue this marriage. Neither one of them is sure that they want to get divorced. So Gladys has gone to see an attorney and Pete has gone to see you and both sides have agreed to meet and negotiate the terms of separation. What is the first thing you are going to say to Pete? You want to focus on his interests in preparation for the negotiation so why don't you start with some questions: *What do you want to accomplish in this negotiation, Pete? What are your goals?*

Pete tells you that he still loves his wife and he doesn't want to get a divorce. He also tells you that he knows he can't stop the separation but he doesn't know how he is going to live outside of the house. He can't afford two households. Those are Pete's interests. Pretty simple. Pretty clear. What do you do next? Why not ask Pete what he thinks Gladys wants to accomplish. He will probably initially say something like, "She wants to rake me over the coals" but you know he doesn't mean that and, eventually, you get him focusing on Gladys' interests.

"She wants to have enough money to run the household."

"I know, Pete, but let's dig a little deeper. She has enough money now and she's not happy."

"That's true. I think she feels trapped. She loves her kids but she wants to get out of the house. She wants to pursue her career. She has a bachelor's in education but she's knee deep in diapers and laundry and crying kids."

About this time, if you're listening, you're probably realizing that Pete really does love his wife and he's a pretty perceptive guy. He just got caught in his own trap.

"Do you think she still loves you?"

"I do. But what's love got to do with it when you are in so much pain?"

About now, if you are my age, you've got a rock and roll song going on in your head: *What's love got to do, got to do with it? What's love but a second-hand emotion?* You dismiss the song immediately. This is no time for levity.

So, if Pete is right, Gladys still loves him but she's caught in a trap. She wants to pursue her own life. Now that we have established at least what we think are both parties' interests, where do we go from here?

"Got any ideas how to satisfy Gladys' needs?"

"I've been thinking about that since we've been married. I keep trying but it just gets worse. We're both lost."

"Do you have any family here?"

"My mother is here. Her parents are here."

"Do they work?"

"No. They are all retired."

"Would they be willing to watch the kids and are they able?"

"I think so. They babysit now and then."

"Do your parents and Gladys' parents get along with each other?"

"Yeah. They like each other."

An idea is forming in your brain. *What if we get the grandparents involved in babysitting? They could work out a schedule. And if Gladys could go to work and not have the cost of daycare maybe she could get a housekeeper to clean the house and do the wash. What else is out there?*

You and Pete talk about potential solutions for a couple of more hours. Then you send Pete home with some homework.

"I want a list of all your bills. I want to know all the income you have from any source. I want you to talk to your mother about helping out with daycare needs. Find out exactly what she is willing to do. And I want you to start looking for accommodations you can live with for at least six months."

So you have explored both Pete and Gladys' interests, you've explored potential solutions to satisfy those interests, and you've made Pete do his homework so you can discuss the specifics. One more meeting to go over the numbers and you are probably ready to sit down and negotiate.

Let's go back to Art now. How does he prepare for his negotiation with George? Well, we know how the opening is going to go. What does Art want to do after that? Again, if you were representing Art you might want to ask him some questions.

"What are your goals in this negotiation?"

"First, and foremost," Art tells you, "I want to put this baby to bed. The longer George Deely is out there, the bigger this headache is going to get."

"Are you willing to pay whatever he is asking?"

"Just about. But I still want to get the best deal."

"And in your mind, what is the best deal?"

"Fifty thousand dollars. That pays for the damaged furniture but it is the lower evaluation of the painting's value. I don't think I can make an offer lower than that without making George angry all over again."

"What about George? What do you think he wants?"

"I think he wants to be treated with respect. That's why I think I should apologize at the outset of the negotiation. He probably wants his painting back as well although that's impossible. I think we need to talk about that. And, in the end, he probably wants as much money as he can get and he has given us that number. It's $80,000."

Art is probably right on. If he can deal with the emotional issue, and that is a significant issue, he can probably get the case settled between $50,000 and $80,000.

Let's take another scenario and this time let's dig a little deeper. And we will leave the attorneys out of the discussion for the moment.

Jane is the Chief Operating Officer of a start-up company. Before beginning her employment, she negotiated her compensation package that included her salary, a bonus structure, an ownership interest, a non-compete clause, and a severance package. Two months into the job, Jane realized that her boss, the CEO (we'll call him Wes which is short for Weasel), was a micromanager, nitpicking everything she did and undermining her with the employees she supervised. After several conversations with this idiot to no avail, Jane realized that she was living a nightmare and she had to get out. Unfortunately, her severance package didn't kick in until she was at the company for six months. If she left after six months, she would get a year's salary. Her bonus (of up to one year's salary) did not kick in until six months had passed as well. If she was fired in the first six months, she would get her salary and a portion of her bonus unless she was fired for cause. If she was fired for cause, she got nothing. Jane knew that if she stayed for six months she would be a basket case and her compensation package would barely cover her psychiatrist's bills. On the other hand, she couldn't just walk away without another job.

This isn't the usual situation for a negotiation in the sense that both parties want to sit down and discuss a resolution of some issue between them such as, say, the original compensation package Jane negotiated with the start-up company. Then, they were interested in her and she was interested in them, and the process consisted of nailing down the terms of employment. Here, it's not so simple. For instance, what would be the probable outcome if Jane walked into Wes' office and said in a very straightforward way, "I can't do this anymore. I want out. I would like to negotiate the terms of my departure"? Wes, the sweetheart that he seemed to be, would probably say something like "Ok, here is my proposal. You turn around and walk out that door you came in and do it quickly so it doesn't close and hit you in an embarrassing place."

The straightforward is not going to work simply because Jane has no leverage. By the way, you would be surprised to know that most people would do exactly what they should not do: that is, walk into Wes' office and attempt to negotiate *before sitting down and actually contemplating what they want to do and how they want to do it.* That would be the spur-of-the-moment thing to do and it would be the wrong thing to do as well.

Jane needs to map her situation out from A to Z before she ever starts the negotiation. And she needs to start by identifying her interests. In Jane's case, money *appears to be* the only solution because Jane can't leave without getting her severance package: She doesn't have another job and can't live too long without another paycheck. But is money Jane's primary interest? If it was she could wait six months and get her severance. No. Jane's main interest is getting away from Wes as soon as possible to save her sanity. Jane's secondary interest is getting her severance package or a portion of it, including her bonus, so that she can live while looking for another job. What else? Could she continue at the company and just not work for Wes? It's a possibility, but one Jane does not want to entertain, because Wes would still be the driving force for the company and Jane does not see his vision for the Company being a successful one. She left her prior job to go with a start-up company primarily because she wanted to be a part of creating something and she wanted to *own* a part of that creation. Staying at a company that Wes was running, even if she were not working directly under him, would not satisfy her interests at all.

So Jane has identified her interests in preparation for her negotiation with Wes, the Weasel. What else does "the Necessary" entail for her to be fully prepared for her meeting with Wes? Well, wouldn't it be helpful if Jane could identify Wes' interests? And why would she want to do that? If she could give something to Wes to satisfy his interests, then the likelihood of reaching a settlement would increase substantially. Alternatively, even if she couldn't give something to Wes, if she knew his motives, it might help her to develop an exit negotiation strategy. But how does Jane go about figuring out what Wes' interests are? Does she go to a palm reader or a soothsayer? They can theoretically tell the future but can they actually tell her about the interests of somebody else they have never met? It may depend on how much money Jane has in her pocket, but probably not.

Jane can do this herself, though—if she works at it. Jane knows more than she thinks she does. For instance, Jane knows that Wes has been criticizing her for her work performance and Jane knows that Wes has been undermining her behind her back with her fellow employees. She also knows from her interactions with him that Wes does not particularly like her. Jane likes to be liked, but in this particular instance she does not feel bad because Wes makes her stomach turn every time she has a conversation with him.

Wes and the Company paid Jane an awful lot of money to come work for them, including a piece of the pie, so Wes did not start out disliking Jane or her work. And if he was not satisfied with her work why did he not just tell her and end the charade? Why was he nitpicking and undermining her with her fellow employees? Well, Wes has shareholders he has to answer to. Some of the shareholders were involved in the negotiations to get Jane. They are not going to be happy if she goes and they are definitely not going to be happy if she goes with a year's salary plus a bonus. If she, at least, left without costing the company money, Wes could sell her departure a lot easier. How could Wes get out of this contract with Jane free and clear? If Jane left the Company of her own accord before six months passed, the Company would not owe her any money. Or, if Jane was fired for cause, the Company would not have to pay her any money. Looking at Wes' behavior in light of those objectives, what he was doing made perfect sense. Wes had decided that Jane was not the person for the job and then was proceeding to make life so miserable for her she would quit. And, alternatively, if she didn't quit, Wes was probably documenting all his nitpicking sessions with her and undermining her with her fellow employees so he could fire her for cause before the six months was up.

Now, at least, everything made sense for Jane. By sitting down and thinking about it and looking at things through Wes' lens, Jane could see what his interests were. They certainly didn't have any coinciding interests, so how was this new knowledge going to aid Jane in her negotiation with Wes?

So far, we have discussed the concepts of identifying not only your client's interests in preparation for a negotiation but also the interests of the other party. Since Jane and Wes are so at odds with each other, we were only able to identify competing interests. They do have one interest in common, though: They both want Jane to leave as soon as possible. How does Jane use that knowledge to her advantage? What else needs to be done in the preparation process before Jane is ready to sit down with Wes and negotiate her exit from the Company? In most situations, you would want to spend some time identifying possible solutions. Like interests, solutions are not as obvious as they may seem. For instance, a possible solution in this case would have been for Jane to work under someone else in the Company, but, of course, that solution was not viable for Jane. She has to leave the Company and she has to leave with a severance.

We mentioned previously in this discussion that Jane could not simply barge into Wes' office and state that she wanted out and that she wanted to discuss her severance package because *she had no leverage*. Leverage is called many things in the negotiation teaching field. Some people call it your BATNA (Best Alternative To A Negotiated Settlement), which means simply what happens when I don't reach a settlement, or when do I walk away because the settlement is worse than the alternative.[3] If you have a bad BATNA, you have little or no

---

3. Fisher R., Ury, W. and Patton B. (1991). *Getting To Yes: Negotiating Agreement Without Giving In*. Second Edition, New York: Penguin Books.

negotiating power. Jane has no negotiating power if she walks into Wes' office and says I want to quit, when her contract says she gets nothing if she quits. Just like you have to think about your interests and your opponents' interests while preparing for a negotiation, you also have to think about your BATNA. And if your BATNA is bad, you have to try and make it better. How does Jane make her BATNA better? Or to put it in clearer terms, how does Jane increase her leverage?

By understanding Wes' motives, Jane also understands that she cannot simply sit and wait for six months to pass so she can get her severance. The more time that passes the more opportunity for Wes to "document" her bad performance and work on her employees who are also his employees since he signs the paychecks. Jane has to act now and she has to have a clear strategy.

In all of these hypotheticals, the message about negotiating a possible resolution is thorough preparation. That means taking the time to fully understand your side's needs, wants, motivations, and line in the sand, and taking the time to understand your opponent's as well. Thorough preparation also looks for any leverage or bargaining chips that each side has so you know what you have to work with, may make a demand for, or may have to give up to get the deal done. And this preparation requires you to look deep, beyond just the surface for the obvious. When you do your homework to prepare for negotiation, the outcome can be much more successful as you'll see later in this chapter when we again visit the parties from our hypotheticals.

Stop Points

1. You need to prepare thoroughly for a negotiation.
2. Preparation includes identifying your interests *and* your opponent's interests. Don't stick to the surface. Dig deep.
3. Once you have identified your interest and your opponent's interests, you have to look for solutions. Again, don't be satisfied with the obvious.
4. Do a careful and objective analysis of your bargaining power. If you don't have any leverage, try to get some.

III. The Negotiation

So, we are all prepared. We know what we want and we think we have a bead on what our opponent wants and we have potential solutions. We are ready to begin the negotiation. A couple of things we should keep in mind before we start: Patience is a virtue. It takes people a long time to change their mind. Every negotiation has its own flow. Try and feel that flow. *Feel* when it is the right time to make a particular offer. Don't be too impatient. Be open and be flexible. Things never turn out the way you planned them. The other side may have some good ideas. Remember your goals. Remember your BATNA. Don't make a bad deal just for the sake of making a deal.

Since we have already discussed Art's opening statement in great detail, let's start with Art and George. Art and the attorneys make small talk because George won't look at Art. And let's just revisit this for a second. Take the time to exchange first names, if possible. Take the time to establish a connection. It can be very helpful.

Okay, small talk is over. Art makes his pitch. "We're sorry. We're sorry. We're sorry. We insulted you with that offer of $125. We're here in good faith to resolve this dispute, etc., etc., etc."

George is genuinely affected by Art's words because Art has looked him in the eye and it is clear to George that Art means what he is saying. Where do we go from here? Art has dissipated the emotional issue but he hasn't made an offer yet *and he doesn't intend to make an offer right away!*

"George, I have read your claim form but I would like to get a little more information on the items of furniture and how you evaluated the damage and I'd like to hear about the painting as well—when you bought it, where you bought it. Is this one of your favorite artist's paintings?"

Art is not just exchanging pleasantries. He's exploring what's out there. What is George really looking for and why? Art has done his homework but he is not really sure what George's interests are, so he is asking. In every negotiation, before the parties start making offers and counteroffers there should be a period of time for fact-finding. Find out what is important to the other side before you start making offers or demands.

George talks about the 3 items in his claim, an antique chair, an antique table, and the painting. He first talks about the antique chair with the broken leg that is irreplaceable. It was a family heirloom. George has placed a value on that of $10,000 with no backup documentation. Next, George describes the antique table that was purchased for $15,000 twenty years ago. George is certain it's worth at least $20,000 now. And finally, George describes the painting, which is a Heras original. Heras is a surrealist with a substantial following in the art world. His work is only going to grow in value. This is the piece that is most important to George. He wants $50,000 for it, even though he only paid $25,000 for it five years ago.

Art now has the information he needs. He knows what George's interests are and he knows what is most important to George. There is no set-in-stone answer as to where he should start, but Art wants to get off on the right foot. He wants to reach agreement on something. He chooses the antique table.

"Do you have any documentation to substantiate the $20,000 figure for the current value of the table?" Art asks. George, as Art suspects, does not have any documentation.

Art starts by creating a little good will. "Okay, I'm going to accept your number because it's logical that an antique would increase in value over twenty years and it's a reasonable number. Now, can we talk about the painting?"

Art wants to leave the chair on the backburner either as a negotiating tool for himself or for George, if necessary.

"I have familiarized myself with Heras' work," Art begins. "A fascinating artist. He reminds me of Dali."

George smiles. Those are his thoughts exactly. "Yes, his work is irreplaceable. No money is going to compensate me for the loss of that painting."

"I understand." Art says. "And I appreciate your sentiments. I'm an art lover myself. But we can't replace that which is irreplaceable, we can only compensate. I have had the painting appraised by two well-known appraisal houses and both have given me the same number. It's not what you are looking for."

Art has given his reasons. He has lowered George's expectations but he has not yet given the number.

"What was the appraisal?" George asks.

"$30,000."

Let's step out of the negotiation for a moment and discuss this counteroffer of Art's. Art gave his reasons first before giving the number. Always give your reasons first. If you are making a demand and it is a high demand, sell it first. Predispose your listener to what is coming so it is not a shock. If it is a shock there will be a corresponding defensive reaction and it is hard to dissipate that negative reaction. Art was lowering expectations and giving his reasons for the offer before he made it. He went so far as to have George ask for the number.

Another thing that Art has done very skillfully is use objective standards. He didn't pull a number out of the air. He got not one but two appraisals from some reputable art appraisers. George may have done his homework as well and come up with some appraisals of his own, but if he hasn't, these objective appraisals are pretty powerful statements that are hard to rebut.

And for the last point, Art knows he probably is going to have to move from the $30,000 number, but this is the lowest place he can start and support with reasons. If he went any lower, George would probably walk out of the room. Whatever side you are on, pick the best position for your client that you can support with reasons. If you go too high or too low, you risk alienating the other side. Starting with your best position leaves you room to negotiate.

"You're only looking at the present," George responds. "That painting, accepting your numbers, has gone up in value $10,000 in five years. Who knows what it will be worth ten years from now."

Art is tempted to say that the future is irrelevant. Insurance only covers present value. But Art understands that a statement like that, although true, will cause George to get angry and defensive and will hinder effective negotiation going forward. He may have to say it at some point but not now. Art needs a deal and he has another proposal for George.

"George, you know that Heras did another painting very similar to the one you lost."

"Yes, *The Gathering*, I'm very familiar with it."

"Would you say it's comparable in value to your lost painting?"

"I'm not sure."

"What if I were to tell you that it is comparable in value and that we can obtain that painting for you. Would that provide a reasonable substitute to you for your loss?"

Here is where George surprises Art. "No. I want to be compensated."

Art now has to regroup. It appears George was not totally forthcoming. It's not about the art, it's about the money.

"Our obligation," Art begins, "is to pay you for the value of the painting on the day it was destroyed. We have tried to take into account your position that this painting is going to increase in value by finding you a comparable painting by the same artist. It too will presumably increase in value. You're not interested in that possibility. I'm not sure where to go from here."

Art has given George the bad news in as nice a way as possible. Of course, he is prepared to give up a lot more but he is throwing the ball back into George's court. George obviously needs money for some reason. How desperate is he?

"I'm not going to accept $30,000," George responds.

"Okay." Art doesn't say anything more. He has made his offer. Silence can sometimes be an effective tool. It's George's turn to counter.

"I will accept $40,000."

Art now knows the full parameter of the playing field.

"Let's talk about this chair for a minute, George. You've put a number out there without any documentation. I see it's a fine piece of furniture and I understand the family sentiments but if we can reach a reasonable number on the chair of $5,000, I'll agree to pay you $40,000 for the painting."

George came into the negotiation ready to accept a few thousand for the chair. The negotiation has gone much better than he ever imagined. He accepts Art's offer.

Art has paid a lot, but he has closed a case that could have been a disaster for the company. He came into the negotiation expecting to pay a lot, but he needed to get George sold on the premise that they could resolve the dispute amicably and then he needed to save as much money as he could. It was a win/win for both sides.

Let's shift gears now and go to Pete and Gladys—a totally different negotiation. You as Pete's attorney have gathered all the information and come up with a strategy to try and meet Pete's interests and Gladys' interests and leave the door open for a future reconciliation. The first thing you have decided to do is let Pete speak directly to Gladys. This is obviously an emotional situation and the two parties need to talk to each other if anything meaningful is going to get done. You have total faith in Pete, but you have gone over his presentation with him several times to make sure that he does not say the wrong thing.

After the pleasantries are exchanged between the lawyers—Pete and Gladys at this point are not exchanging pleasantries—you turn it over to Pete to make his pitch.

"Gladys, as you know, I am not here because I want to be, but I accept that we are going to be separated for awhile. I want to approach this negotiation with the idea that someday we will be reunited. I know these past few years have been hard for you. They have been hard for both of us. Right now, I am not making enough money to maintain two households, but I am agreeing to move out. I have found a small apartment for a reasonable rent and I have a proposed budget that allows me to live very modestly while taking care of your and the kids' needs. I want to go further though. I want to make sure you have time for yourself and time to pursue your own dreams. We have some ideas that we want to present today that will help you to do that. I hope that we can work together to solve these issues."

It's short and sweet and it sets the tone. Gladys' lawyer responds with a typical list of demands. After both sides have stated their positions, Pete's lawyer, you, come out with a spreadsheet that shows exactly what Pete makes, the expenses of the house, the cost of the new apartment, Pete's expenses to live, and the allocation of money to make all of this work.

"There are no secrets here," you say. "This is all the money and these are all the expenses. Pete is about to live a no frills life and, frankly, so are you, Gladys, even though you will be remaining in the house. Nothing will change except the two of you will be living in different places and visitation for the children will have to be more structured. Now, having said that, I'd like to explore some other options that, hopefully, will make life better for everybody. Gladys, I understand that you have a teaching degree, is that correct?"

"That's correct," Gladys says, her arms folded. She's clearly not open to this discussion.

"If you had your druthers, would you rather be working at least part-time?"

"I understand what you're doing," Gladys replies. "You're trying to get me back to work so Pete doesn't have to pay as much. Well, it's not going to work. We've been through this a hundred times. Daycare would be more costly than me working. Until they can go to pre-school I'm going to be home."

You reply, "Gladys, Pete is not trying to get out of anything. He is committed to doing whatever it takes. I was not asking about how it could be done, I was just asking whether you wanted to get out of the house at least on a part-time basis."

"Of course I would, but it's not going to happen. We've been down this road a million times."

You now have your commitment from Gladys that this is what she wants to do. Maybe it is time to unveil the plan. Timing is everything. If you are too quick, it won't work. Take a little more time.

"If we could come up with a plan, would you be willing to try it out?"

"It depends on what it is. I'm not going to agree to anything I don't know about."

You bring Pete back in. "I have talked to my mother. She has agreed to commit up to two and a half days a week to babysitting. If your parents can do the same, and I think they will once they know the circumstances, you could go back to work part-time or full-time depending on what you want to do."

"You just want to save money."

"I'm not going to reduce my payments even if you are working. Now, down the road, if we decide to get divorced, that may be a different story. During this period of separation, if you can get a job and work as a teacher, that money is yours. You can get a housekeeper. You can do whatever you want."

Gladys is starting to get the picture that this is really about her and her happiness. She starts to relax and talk about the details. An agreement is not reached that day because her mom and dad have not been approached, but most of the specifics are nailed down. This would not have happened if you and Pete did not sit down and discuss what Pete wanted, what Gladys needed, and what solutions were out there long before you walked into the negotiating session. It also would not have happened if you moved too quickly or if you assumed things before doing your fact-finding. Even when everything is in their favor, it takes people a long time to change their mind.

Now to the toughest negotiation of the three—Jane's negotiation with Wes, the weasel. On Tuesday, Jane makes an appointment to visit with Wes on Thursday afternoon. The stated purpose is to talk about the company and how things are going. By setting it up that way, Jane is giving Wes time to think about what is going to happen. He probably thinks that she is going to resign. He has stepped up the pressure recently and Jane can feel it. Her employees are starting to ignore her, knowing she has no real power.

Jane wants out and she wants to leave with a year's severance. She knows the bonus is a long shot but she plans to use it as leverage.

The day of the meeting arrives. It takes place in Wes' office where he feels most comfortable and most powerful. Jane is okay with that because she is going to test his power today. There is no small talk between these two. Jane opens the discussion.

"I asked for this meeting because things have not been going well between you and I and it has caused some problems with my employees as well."

"*My* employees," Wes interrupts.

"Yes, your employees. And therein lies the problem. You hired me to be the operations person but you are not letting me do my job. You are trying to be the operations person as well as the CEO and you are undermining my authority in the process."

Wes can't help but smile. This is going exactly as he thought it would.

"Maybe I'm doing your job because you're not doing your job."

"That's what I thought you'd say," Jane replies. "So, I brought some documents with me to this meeting. Since I have been on board, sales have increased each month by ten per cent, so I am doing my job."

Wes still has his smile. She wants to leave but she's making her case for a severance.

"Maybe sales are up because of what I'm doing. I'm talking with your employees every day."

"This can't go on," Jane says.

Smiling Wes, the weasel, asks, "What do you propose?" All the while, he's prepared to tell Jane to hurry through the door so it doesn't whack her on the way out.

"Before I tell you what I propose, I want to tell you what I know—and please don't interrupt. I know that you don't want me here. Your actions have made that clear, including your behavior in this meeting so far. I know that you can fire me, but if you fire me without cause, you have to pay me a year's salary plus my bonus. I believe that you have been meeting with me regularly so you can document issues with my performance. I believe that you are trying to force me to quit or, alternatively, you are documenting your counseling sessions to set up a termination for cause."

"That's ridiculous." The smile has left the weasel's face.

"It may be. It may be all in my mind. I just want to tell you that you can fire me right now. Pay me my severance and my bonus and I will walk out that door. Otherwise, I'm not going anywhere. You're not getting rid of me that easy. And when this meeting is over, I'm sending a letter to the Board of Directors telling them what you have been doing and that you have created a hostile work environment. I would have done it already but I wanted you to know what's coming. You're not going to get away with the game you are playing."

"I'm not playing a game with you. I'm running a business." Wes is a pro. He has not changed his demeanor. Jane is a pro too. She knows she has gotten to him. He does not want the Board of Directors, who are also substantial shareholders, to hear about this.

"I'm part of that business. You hired me to do a job and I believe you are trying to cut me out without paying me what I am due. I left a good job to come here. I believed in you and this company."

"And now you don't."

"I'm not saying that. Things haven't worked out as I planned."

"Where do we go from here?"

"I told you what I'm doing when this meeting is over."

"And where is that going to get you?"

"I may have to stay here for a few more months, but your plan is not going to work, Wes."

"I told you I don't have a plan."

"I heard you. I just don't happen to agree with you."

"What if I agreed to pay you a portion of your severance—four months' salary—if you left today?"

"It would not be acceptable. I'm entitled to my full severance and my bonus."

"Your bonus is discretionary. I could give you a dollar if I chose."

"There was a discussion that my bonus would be up to a year's salary. That language is in the contract."

"Yes. There is a discussion of the maximum limit but not the minimum."

Wes can tell he has made his point. She knows the bonus is discretionary. He can play games with this woman for the rest of the day or he can make her an offer while she is at a disadvantage and try and end the negotiation here.

"I will agree to pay you your severance of one year's salary if you agree to sign a release which will include a non-disparagement clause, today."

"Agreed." Jane says and stands up and shakes Wes' hand before he knows what has happened.

Obviously, most negotiations don't move that quickly or end that satisfactorily. However, if you take the time, like Jane did, to figure things out and, in the process, give yourself some leverage, an outcome like this is more likely than not.

Each of these hypothetical examples are designed to highlight the importance of knowing when to negotiate, how to prepare to negotiate, and then conducting the negotiation itself. Negotiations should not be rushed into without careful thought and preparation. When you are preparing to negotiate, remember that whether it's a domestic issue, an insurance claim, or a business problem, you're dealing with people, and therefore emotions will be at play. Negotiations are never one-sided, so the more you can fully examine each side's positions, interests, emotions, agendas, and motivations, the more likely you will be able to strategize workable and beneficial solutions.

Checkpoints

- Patience is a virtue. It takes people a long time to change their mind.

- Be flexible. Things may not be as you see them. Be prepared to adjust.

- Be open. The other side might have some good ideas of their own.

- Feel the flow. Don't make an offer too quickly or too late. Don't be anxious to get to the end. Find the right time.

- Before you start negotiating, do your fact-finding. Ask questions. Get commitments if possible. Then you are ready to deal.

- Sell it, then tell it. Always give your reasons first. And make sure your reasons have a sound basis.

- Give yourself room to negotiate. Don't make an offer or demand you can't support with reasons, but make the best and highest offer or demand you can support. You can always come down, but you can't go up.

- Don't make a bad deal just to make a deal.

Chapter 3

Mediation

So, what is mediation and why should you be interested in learning mediation? I guess the short answer is: "Mediation is a tool to help resolve disputes. If you're an attorney and you don't know how to negotiate and mediate effectively, you're going to be severely handicapped no matter what field of law you practice in."

Now, I just used the terms "negotiation" and "mediation" in the same sentence. There is a difference between the two, although the elements of a successful negotiation are always present in a mediation. So what is the difference? Negotiation, as we discussed previously in this book, is a more informal process where the parties engage with each other directly. Mediation is much more regulated[1] and introduces a third party into the process: the mediator. Why this third party? There's no simple answer to that question although in most cases a mediator is brought in because the parties are too emotionally involved to negotiate directly or the situation is too adversarial.

In this book, we are going to talk about the mediation process primarily as an arm of the litigation process. Thirty years ago, mediation was virtually nonexistent in litigation. When it was first introduced, most lawyers were not enthusiastic or optimistic about the process. Lawyers looked at mediation as another obstacle on the long journey to the courtroom. But guess what? Mediation revolutionized the litigation process. Now, most cases, an extraordinary number actually, are disposed of or settled in mediation. Cases were settled before mediation came on the scene, but the difficult cases, the complex cases, and the emotional cases were not. So what happened? Why couldn't the lawyers do this on their own?

The simple answer is that in the past lawyers were never trained in the art of negotiation and it was, and still is, very difficult to settle a case that you've been litigating for six months or even several years. But it wasn't just the lawyers. Clients didn't want to settle either. Before mediation, clients for the most part had no involvement in the lawsuit until trial, other than to have their deposition taken. And clients usually had and still have unreasonable expectations about the value of their case, especially unsophisticated clients. Under those circumstances, it was hard for lawyers to get their clients to agree to settle a case. And sometimes the attempt was more trouble than it was worth.

To better understand mediation, let's look at it through a case. Mary Thompson was involved in a car accident with Sam Hanson on July 4 of last year. Mary was driving through an intersection on a green light when she was hit on the driver's side by Sam's car. As a result of the accident, Mary sustained injuries to her neck, back, and left arm and her face suffered cuts and bruises from her air bag.

When Mary first came to see you, her lawyer, the case looked like it was going to be a six-figure case. However, over time, most of Mary's injuries

---

1. In Florida, for instance, the process for mediation is codified in Chapter 44 of the Florida Statutes.

healed, including her facial cuts. The only injury remaining was the injury to Mary's back and her own physician, after doing extensive tests, has opined that she has a disc bulge, which, although painful, will resolve over time and is not considered a serious injury.

Obviously, the value of the case has gone down. You know this and so does the other lawyer but Mary doesn't. It's been just three months since her accident and Mary is still hurt and treating regularly with her doctors. How do you think she'd react if you, her attorney, call her up and say, "I just got an offer on your case for $50,000." Mary might not say it but she just might be thinking, *You mean my case that is worth at least two hundred fifty thousand dollars? Have you just sold me out so you can get a fee and move on to the next case? What's the number of the Bar Association? Maybe I will call and file a complaint.*

But instead of saying all those things that she is thinking, Mary asks you, her lawyer, "What do you think?" What did Shakespeare say—"Ay, there's the rub." How do you respond? Do you say, "I think it's a good settlement. I think you should take it." How do you think that advice is going to be received?

"But I've been injured severely."

"I know you feel that way but a disc bulge is really not a serious injury and it will resolve a lot over time."

Mary's thought process has now advanced to—*That's not what you told me when I came in your office and you wanted my case. Then it was a great case. You're pressuring me. Now I'm definitely calling the Bar Association.*

How does that same situation resolve through mediation? You, the plaintiff's lawyer, have still made the assessment about the case and if you've kept Mary apprised, you've probably told her about some of the issues that will affect what she ultimately will receive. However, you haven't sat down and talked numbers with her because, so far, it hasn't been necessary. Therefore, she probably still has unreasonable expectations about the value of her case. You're still her warrior, her knight in shining armor ready to go forth on the field of battle and shed some blood for her cause. And you go into mediation all suited up with your sword and your lance at the ready. You are polite to the mediator and to the other side but you let them know you are prepared to go the distance—to do whatever it takes. You tell the mediator Mary's story. How she was wronged by the actions of the defendant and how she has suffered because of those actions and you make your demand for damages, a demand that you will stand firm on and fight for no matter what the consequences.[2]

---

2. Your demand is probably for more than the $50,000 offer which you consider reasonable and that is because you never demand what you are willing to accept, a concept that we will discuss later.

Mary is so proud and confident.

Now we have to pause here as we set this scene because there is another side or sides to this mediation, and there are lawyers on the other side and they have clients too, clients who see them as their warriors as well, although it might be a significantly different perspective. A defense lawyer has even more issues to contemplate because, oftentimes, defense clients are not one and done deals. Those clients are the lifeblood of your firm's business and if a defense client does not have confidence in you as its warrior, it will do one of two things: It will go find another firm, or it will ask the managing partner to remove you from the case. Neither option is good for you. And if it happens more than once, you are probably going to be looking for another job. So, this is a high stakes game on both sides and there are a lot of issues that have little to do with the ultimate settlement.

You, the defense lawyer, have discussed the issues with your, in most cases, more sophisticated client. Here that client is Sam's automobile insurance, ABC Insurance Company and its adjuster.[3] Because you have been upfront about ABC's exposure and because your client has been in similar battles before, you have developed a strategy. Your client already knows that there are going to have to be some concessions made. The question is where do you draw the line in the sand. You, the lawyer, may have different thoughts about that than your client, but you both have decided together not to be confrontational at the outset. You have decided not to react to plaintiff counsel's inflammatory rhetoric. Instead, you direct your remarks to Mary directly, something you've been unable to do through the entire litigation process up to this moment. You took Mary's deposition but you were asking questions, seeking information. You weren't having a conversation. You're not having a conversation now, but your *tone* is conversational.

"Ms. Thompson, we know that you were injured in that car accident with our client Mr. Hanson, and we know this has caused you some hardships, and we're sorry that this accident ever happened. We're here in good faith to reach a settlement if we can. However, even though you were injured and have suffered hardships as a result, that does not mean my client is legally responsible. We have legal defenses to your negligence claim and we have expert testimony that disputes the seriousness of your injuries going forward. Again, that does not diminish the fact that you were injured. We regret that. But most of your

---

3. Most people have auto insurance and when they are involved in an accident the insurance company handles the claim, which means that it is assigned to an adjuster who makes the decision as to whether to settle and for how much.

injuries have resolved. These are legal defenses. You need to know about them and the mediator needs to know about them."

Think about Mary's reaction to this. Years ago before mediation was so prevalent, you, as Mary's lawyer, would have explained any issues or downsides of her case to her yourself. You would have received ABC's settlement offer and sat down with Mary to consider it reasonably in light of all the facts and circumstances. But here at mediation, Mary is hearing these "issues and downsides" from the opponent. Where she would be wary and untrusting of you, her own lawyer, if you suggested she accept the settlement offer, in mediation she is hearing it from the other side. You, her lawyer, are still there protecting her. Later, when the mediator starts asking questions of you and Mary, Mary begins to see firsthand that a disinterested third party, the mediator, is questioning the seriousness of her injuries. She starts to see that maybe her case isn't as strong as she thinks it is.

That's why mediation is so special and so successful. It brings the clients into the process. It makes them participate and forces them to see things differently and make the hard decisions. Before, it was always about the lawyers, and the pressure they exerted, and the decisions they forced the clients to make. No longer. The clients are there. The clients are making the decisions. And if you, the lawyer, do your job the right way, your client will be a satisfied client as you walk out the door at the end of the day whether you have a deal or not.

I. Mediators

There is still a great deal to talk about, particularly with regard to the process of mediation, but let us complete this scenario so you, at least, get a feel at the outset of this discussion as to why mediation is so worthwhile. Opening statements have been made. The gauntlet has been laid down. Now it's the mediator's turn to take these parties and their positions, which seem diametrically opposed, and make them move towards each other. How does the mediator do that?

First of all, who is this mediator and how does one attain the vaulted position of mediator? The simple answer is that where you live determines who can and cannot become a mediator. Rules regarding mediation and mediators are statewide and mediation unlike negotiation is much more formalized. However, with the caveat that you must look to the rules of the state where you reside, there are some general principles that we can discuss about who can and cannot become a mediator.

In most states, you do not have to be a lawyer to be a certified mediator. You do, however, have to take a course, usually a forty-hour course, and observe other mediators before you can be certified. No rule is ever that simple though. Law students know there is always an exception, and oftentimes exceptions to the exception. Without exceptions and caveats and grey areas, law school would be a breeze. The exception, when we are talking about mediators, is that the parties can choose to have a non-certified mediator with no training and experience preside over their mediation. Of course, if they don't get the case settled and it is in litigation, the judge might order a second mediation and this time the judge might select the mediator.

Why would you want a certified mediator anyway? *Wouldn't a lawyer with thirty or forty years of experience in litigation who has tried hundreds of cases like mine be just as good?* Maybe. But good litigators don't necessarily make good mediators. If he or she is trying a lot of cases, that means they are not settling their own cases. A lawyer with thirty or forty years of experience who is also a certified mediator would seem to be a perfect choice, but you never know. Mediation, like medicine, is an art, not a science. There are very good mediators out there resolving complex cases who don't even have a law degree. The best you can say is that a certified mediator is probably better than a non-certified mediator. And a certified mediator with experience litigating in the subject matter of the litigation is probably better than a certified mediator unfamiliar with this type of litigation. Of course, law students are inquisitive and ask the question—Why? And they never accept the simple answer. They keep asking why.

So the question is out there—why is a certified mediator probably better than a non-certified mediator even if the non-certified mediator is more experienced in the litigation process? The answer is that the certified mediator has been trained in a very intense training environment in the art and technique of negotiation and settlement. And here's a fundamental concept you as a young lawyer need to understand: to be a good litigator and be successful in the mediation process, you need to understand the fundamentals of negotiation. Why? For one, as we discussed previously, mediation is negotiation with a third party involved. More important, however, the mediator's fundamental training is in the art of negotiation and if you understand what the mediator is doing and the tools he or she is using to try and bring the parties together, you will probably be very successful in the mediation process.

So what kind of training does the mediator receive? Mediators are generally trained using the Harvard method of negotiation that stresses cooperation not confrontation: Separate the people from the problem; identify the interests of the parties; search for solutions for mutual gain; use objective standards.[4] Remember our discussion previously about Mary's lawyer being her warrior and

---

4. *Getting to Yes*, Roger Fisher and William Vry, Penguin Books, Third Edition, 2011.

the defendant's lawyer needing to prove to ABC Insurance that she's a fighter as well? It's pretty hard to identify the other side's interests and search for solutions for mutual gain when you're playing the part of the warrior. That's where the mediator comes in. The mediator receives training in the concepts of negotiation and how to utilize the concepts to get the parties to move closer together until hopefully they can resolve their differences. Understanding the concepts yourself so you can understand what the mediator is doing, or attempting to do, gives you a definitive advantage in the mediation process.

Mediators are also trained in the *process* of mediation. As a general rule, the mediator controls the process. The parties ultimately control whether they are going to settle but the process of determining how they get to that ultimate decision is set by the mediator. It's probably best to talk about the mediator and the process at the same time.

How do the parties choose a mediator, or do they choose a mediator? In most states, mediation as part of the civil litigation process is not mandatory as a matter law but it is as a matter of fact. What does that mean? It means that if the parties don't contemplate mediation as part of their litigation plan, the court will order it for you. Judges love mediation. Cases get settled at mediation, which means trials go away, which means judges' dockets become less cluttered with cases that need to be tried. That's why if you haven't been to mediation by the time you appear before the judge for a pre-trial hearing to schedule a trial date, she is probably going to send you to mediation. The bad part about that process is the court will choose the time for mediation *and*, in some cases, the mediator. If you recognize the reality of mediation in litigation you can, at least, control the time and the person who will conduct the mediation. Lawyers can usually agree on a mediator for a variety of reasons: First and foremost, they don't want the court to, and second, experienced lawyers know who is good and who isn't, and there are enough good people to choose from that agreement on who to use is normally not a problem. So, as a practical matter, remember, if you get to pre-trial and you haven't been to mediation, it's a good bet that the court will order you to go and probably select your mediator.

What we haven't discussed yet, and maybe this is the appropriate spot to talk about it, is the procedure in federal court. Federal courts usually require mediation in most civil cases although, again, it is technically not mandatory. Local rules control the mediation process in federal court but, in general, mediators in federal court are required to be lawyers and usually lawyers who have been in practice for at least ten years.[5] Certain judges prefer certain mediators

---

5. For example, Local Rules for the Middle District of Florida, Chapter Nine. Court Annexed Mediation.

and you should be aware of that preference when choosing a mediator. Also, in federal court lawyers have to come up with a case management plan before they start discovery.[6] The case management plan is basically a schedule of discovery for a particular case made by the lawyers: When depositions are going to be taken; when dispositive motions are going to be filed; when pre-trial and trial are going to occur; *and when mediation is going to take place.* You'll notice I didn't say *if* mediation is going to take place, I said *when* mediation is going to take place. Get yourself in that mindset.

Mediation is an incredibly helpful process to resolve disputes, but to be a successful process, you need to consider who would be the best mediator for that client in that case. Do you want someone with experience in the same expertise that the claim involves, or a mediator with a firm but kind way of talking to clients? Do you want a mediator who is certified or one who is a non-lawyer?

Choosing who will conduct the mediation can be crucial to how well the mediation proceeds. If you get the wrong person, say someone who doesn't want to put the hard work in to get the case settled, or someone ready to quit at a moment's notice, then you and your client will have lost a golden opportunity to get the matter resolved.

Stop Points

1. Judges prefer mediation to trial. Therefore in most jurisdictions, even where mediation is not mandatory, judges will refer you to mediation before setting the case for trial.
2. If you voluntarily decide to go to mediation, you can control when to go and who the mediator will be.
3. Lawyers can generally agree on a mediator.
4. In mediation, the parties are much more involved in the outcome since they are the decision makers.
5. Mediators control the process of mediation.
6. Mediators are usually trained and certified. In most jurisdictions, you don't have to be a lawyer to be a mediator.
7. It's generally better to mediate with a certified mediator and a mediator experienced in the subject matter of the dispute.

---

6. Federal Rules of Civil Procedure, Rule 26(f).

A. Timing

So when is the best time to go to mediation? Everybody has different thoughts about this and while we're discussing it, it's good to keep in mind that you may go to mediation more than once in a given case. If you go to mediation early and it doesn't settle, the judge may order you back to mediation before you go to trial. The parties can agree to a second mediation but, in most cases, it's the judge who orders it. Again, when is the most appropriate time? The answer is, as it so often is in legal matters, it depends. If you have a good case, and you know the lawyer on the other side, or even if you don't know the lawyer on the other side, you may just call him or her up and say, "Why don't we go to mediation before I file suit. Let's see if we can settle this without litigation." Why would you do that? For one, it saves money. Litigation is very, very expensive. Let me say that again: Litigation is very, very expensive. Also, if the parties know each other, early mediation prevents further acrimony. Think of Gladys and Pete, who tried separation, but decide to get divorced. The earlier they settle their differences, the sooner they can get on with their lives. And because they have children, that means dealing with each other forever. So, the shorter the battle, the better off everybody is. That's why pre-suit mediation is so popular in divorce cases, although, in many situations, some discovery has to occur to understand what and where all the assets are.

Here is a fundamental thought to keep in mind: You can mediate at any time. If you've done enough discovery to know the good and bad of both sides, then maybe it's time to mediate and save some money. If you get to a point where further litigation is going to cause further harm to one side or both, maybe it's time to mediate.

In a recent Whistleblower case, a lawyer filed a Motion For a Temporary Restraining Order to have his client, Megan, reinstated to her former position. The lawyer's chances of winning that Motion were slim but he needed to get the Defendant to state in detail all the reasons for Megan's termination at the earliest possible moment to lock the Defendant into its "story." "Stories" change, especially in Whistleblower cases, as the evidence changes. You have to lock people in early. The lawyer's vehicle for doing that was this Motion For a Temporary Restraining Order, although he did have some hope that he could win and have Megan reinstated. The day the Response was to be filed, defense counsel emailed the Response to Megan's lawyer and suggested that the parties agree to an extension before it was actually filed. The purpose was three-fold: On the one hand, defense counsel wanted to let Megan's lawyer know the Company had a strong case. On the other hand, simply by proposing the delay, he also wanted to let the lawyer know very subtly that he thought the Company might have some problems, particularly if discovery did not support the company's "story." Last, and most important, there were many disparaging statements about Megan in that response, which would be a public record if filed. Whether Megan would ultimately be successful in the litigation, that pleading would be a public record for a long time and available for every future prospective employer to see. What a great incentive for both sides to go to mediation at that juncture. After the lawyer discussed the Response with Megan, which did take a few days because there were emotions involved, Megan agreed to try mediation.

The case ultimately settled because of the timing of the mediation. Both parties could see enough of the other side's case to know they each could lose, and both parties also knew that they would suffer damage no matter what, if they continued the litigation. Most cases aren't so clear. It's the lawyer's job to always be considering when the moment is best to mediate.

The timing of when mediation should occur often depends on what type of case you have and what court you are in. For instance, most employment cases in federal court are decided on summary judgment and most employment cases are decided against the plaintiff. So, let's say the plaintiff, Norman, has a retaliation case. He says he reported sexual harassment and a year later, his employer fired him. He's got some evidence to support his case but certainly not overwhelming evidence. The employer, on the other hand, states that Norman was fired for legitimate business reasons totally unrelated to the report of sexual harassment. When is the best time to mediate that case? Of course, the parties could have attempted mediation before trial but the employer would probably offer nuisance value, which is a small amount to get rid of the case. Something might come up during discovery that might prompt both parties to suggest mediation but that is a rare occurrence. What about after discovery is completed? After discovery is completed is usually the best time for mediation in both state and federal court because both sides usually have a little fear. No case is perfect and discovery usually uncovers the weaknesses of each side's case. Theoretically, that would be the perfect time for mediation and it usually is.

However, when you are in federal court and you have an employment case where most defendants win on summary judgment, what's going to happen if you attempt to mediate after discovery has ended but before the court rules on the dispositive summary judgment motion? The defendant is going to be sitting there thinking—"I'm not going to be offering too much because I've got a great chance of getting out of this case on summary judgment." What are the chances of getting that case settled for a reasonable amount under those circumstances? Not very good. Now, let's say you go to mediation in the same case *after* discovery has been completed *and after* the summary judgment motion has been decided in plaintiff's favor. The parties are now on equal footing again. The next door they are going to open is the courtroom door. The plaintiff thinks he has a good case but knows there are pitfalls. The defendant feels the same way. Isn't this the ideal time for mediation in that case?

So again, mediation can be an incredibly helpful way to resolve disputes, but to be most successful, you must decide when to mediate. Based on your client and the details of the claim, an early mediation may be beneficial and have more chance of success than a later one. However, mediation doesn't have to just take place once; parties can participate in mediation at numerous times during a claim including before a lawsuit is filed, after a lawsuit is filed, and before a trial is set. However, the court is more likely to be involved in subsequent mediations and that may reduce your ability to choose the time and place and, most importantly, the mediator. So lawyers should carefully consider when the first mediation should take place to most benefit their clients.

Stop Point

1. The decision when to mediate depends on the facts and circumstances of each case.

B. Process

Let's return to our discussion of process: The mediator has no say over whether the parties settle or not. The mediator is not a judge or an arbitrator—she does not decide any issue in the case. Nor should she raise issues that the parties themselves have not brought to the table. The mediator's job is simply to be a facilitator. However, the mediator does control the process as I have said numerous times already. *What does that mean?*

For one, it means that the mediator sets the tone—even creates the atmosphere. If you go to a successful mediator's office, you will find that the mediation rooms are decorated and furnished in such a way that the participants feel comfortable—as close to being in their own living room as a business office can be. There's usually finger food and plenty of water, coffee, and soda to drink. A good mediator also knows that it takes time for people to change their minds but that long lunch breaks are not conducive to keeping the ball rolling towards settlement. So, at the appropriate time, lunch will arrive with enough variety to satisfy even the most finicky eater, and, while the parties eat, the mediation continues.

Let's say the mediation begins at 9 A.M. sharp. The mediator is there to greet you and take you to the room where the mediation is to take place. If you're early and want to talk to your client beforehand, she may usher you to a smaller room. At the appropriate time, the mediator will assemble everybody in the mediation room to talk about the ground rules—*the process* of mediation. This initial opening by the mediator is also an informal conversation even though it's required by law and the information conveyed is required by law to be conveyed to the parties. The mediator will usually start by *welcoming* the parties to mediation, stressing that this is an opportunity for both parties to control their own destiny. You will hear these words over and over in mediation in one form or another:

"Mediation is an opportunity for you to control your own destiny. If you don't take this opportunity your case is going to be decided by a third party, either a judge or a jury. In either event, and I'm sure your lawyers have told you this, the outcome is uncertain *no matter how strong you believe your case is.* You have an opportunity today to take your case out of the hands of those third parties and end the uncertainty. You most likely will not get everything you want. Both sides have to give. But, if I do my job and you do your job, you will leave here with a settlement you can live with."

That part of the mediator's opening statement, sets the tone for the mediation. It's very important for the clients to hear that statement. It empowers them but it also puts pressure on them to move—*to give.* Remember at the outset of this discussion we talked about the client being part of the mediation process. It begins right here. Throughout the mediation, the pressure is going to be on the clients to make decisions—*and concessions*—so at the conclusion, no matter what the outcome, the clients feel that they've been part of the process. You will hear from time to time—*my lawyer sold me down the river*—but, if the client has been involved in a good mediation, *and has made the concessions herself,* those words will be replaced by statements like: *It was a battle. We didn't get everything we wanted. But it was a good settlement.* The operative words in that statement are "*we.*" Mediation, first and foremost, brings the client into the process.

By the way, this is true also for the "seasoned" defense client. The classic example of a seasoned defense client is ABC Insurance Company's adjuster assigned to Sam's claim. In most cases involving insurance companies, it's the adjuster who holds the purse strings. In the past, the adjuster had to rely on reports from the lawyer and the opinions of the lawyer. Now, the adjuster attends the mediations and can eyeball the plaintiff, Mary, hear from Mary, and evaluate Mary as a potential witness. The adjuster can also hear the arguments first-hand from Mary's attorney. Thus, the adjuster too feels much more a part of the process than in the past.

What else does the mediator say in that opening statement? Well, the mediator has to tell the parties what mediation is. That explanation would go something like this:

"Mediation is a process where the parties, you folks, come before me, the mediator, and I as a facilitator try and help you reach a resolution of the issues in dispute. This is an informal process. You, the parties are the decision makers. I will help you identify issues, and explore settlement alternatives but the ultimate decisions are yours. Does everybody understand that?"

The mediator also needs to advise the parties that she's not a judge or an arbitrator and she is not going to decide anything. The attorneys are certainly free to talk about the legal issues and the mediator may ask questions to test the legal theories, but she's not going to issue any rulings. Now in some states if the parties agree and request it, the mediator can give a binding or a non-binding opinion on an issue. That is not mediation, though: it's arbitration. In states like Florida, the mediator would not be able to give an opinion in the middle of the mediation even though the parties requested it. She would have to adjourn the mediation. Then, if the parties desired, she could decide a legal issue as an arbitrator. This is a very slippery slope for mediators and, in almost all cases, the mediator will try to stick to the role of facilitator.

The mediator also has to discuss confidentiality in her opening statement. What is confidentiality in the context of a mediation? Simply put, it means anything that is said both orally or in writing by anyone who attends the mediation, not just the parties, is confidential and cannot be disclosed outside of the mediation room. There are two types of confidentiality in a mediation: What the parties say to each other in joint session and what the parties say to the mediator in private sessions.

Let's break that down: Almost every mediation begins in joint session. It does not have to be that way. If the mediator feels that a joint session would not be conducive to reaching a settlement agreement because the parties are too hostile towards each other, she may start out with the parties in separate rooms. It would mean giving two opening statements, but if it keeps the parties from growing further apart and facilitates a settlement, it's worth it. Let's assume, however, that the parties begin in joint session, as they do in most cases. Everything that is said in that joint session is confidential and the mediator has to inform the parties of that confidentiality at the outset of the mediation. The purpose of confidentiality is to allow the parties to speak freely in mediation without the other side using what is said against that party in further proceedings down the road if the case is not settled. That confidentiality is very effective. It's very similar to the evidentiary rule that settlement discussions in general are not admissible because the court wants to encourage parties to settle and if those discussions could be introduced at trial or in motion hearings for any reason, the parties wouldn't have those discussions. It's just common sense.

Confidentiality goes further than that, however. Confidentiality covers more than admissibility in further court proceedings: the parties are precluded from discussing what happened at mediation to anyone at any time. And the statute mandating confidentiality may also provide for damages if that confidentiality is breached. The attorneys take these rules very seriously but the clients normally don't. They go home and tell everybody what happened. It's usually not a problem but every once in a while it becomes one. So, as the attorney, make clear to your client what is potentially at stake if they breach that confidentiality. If the breach comes back to bite them, at least, they won't be able to look at you and say, "You didn't warn me. You didn't make it clear. I didn't understand."

The other type of confidentiality is the confidentiality that attaches when the parties are in private session. What do I mean by private session? After the mediator has concluded her opening remarks and the parties have made their opening statements, the mediator will usually split the parties up. Either the plaintiff or the defendant will go to another room. I say usually because sometimes it doesn't happen. Sometimes the mediator feels that more can be accomplished by keeping the parties together for awhile either because she wants to ask some questions while everyone is in the room, or the parties are talking and she doesn't want to stop the communication, or for a variety of other reasons. However, in most cases, the parties are split up after the opening statements and the mediator shuffles from room to room. The meetings with each party are the private sessions referred to earlier. They are normally called caucuses. Those private sessions are confidential.

Of course, some of what is said in those private sessions has to be conveyed to the other side or there would be no mediation. In fact, most of what is said in private session is communicated to the other side. The mediator handles this in one of two ways: She will either say to the party she is meeting with, "I'm going to assume everything you tell me I can convey to the other side and, if there is something you don't want me to convey, I want you to specifically tell me that." Or she will say, "I'm going to assume everything you tell me is confidential and I want you to specifically tell me what I can convey to the other side." Again, in most cases, since most everything is going to be communicated, the mediator puts the obligation on the party to tell her specifically what it does not want communicated to the other side.

So, to recap: A mediator in her opening statement has to explain to the parties what mediation is, what her role as a mediator is, that the mediation is confidential and what confidentiality means. What happens after that?

We have already touched on this a little: After the mediator gives her opening statement, the parties have an opportunity to give opening statements. What do you want to say in that opening statement? Is it as formal as an opening statement in a courtroom before a judge or a jury? The answer to that question, once again, is: it depends. It depends on what you want to accomplish. There have been mediations where the plaintiff's lawyer has brought videos, charts, anatomical parts, and has put on a show even greater than any opening a judge would allow in court. Most openings in mediation, however, are rather informal. They are aimed at giving the mediator the information she needs to get started. And, in most cases, they are aimed at sending a message to the other side. The elaborate opening I just discussed was clearly meant to send a message to the other side that the jury is going to see all of this and it is going to make a difference.

Let me digress for a moment: In most states, the parties can provide the mediator with a confidential mediation statement prior to mediation. The purpose of the mediation statement is to apprise the mediator of the issues from each party's perspective and to let the mediator know if there have been any settlement discussions prior to mediation and, if so, what those settlement discussions were. Most attorneys who take the time to do a mediation statement also want to convince the mediator of the righteousness of their cause and tell the mediator why they should win. Try to avoid this temptation. Remember, mediators are not there to decide anything. Sure, a well-prepared mediation statement could predispose the mediator to think you have the better case. But that does not mean that you argue your case in the mediation statement. It does not mean that you prepare a brief on the legal issues. If you want to apprise the mediator of a controlling case, that would be appropriate, but don't go beyond that. Your mediation statement should be brief and to-the-point. It should tell the mediator where you are in the litigation process; the issues involved in the case; and what settlement discussions have taken place to date.

Mediation statements are very helpful if the issues are complex. They give the mediator a jump on the process so she doesn't have to spend too much time understanding what the case is about. If the case is a simple one, mediation statements are less helpful. There is no downside, however, to providing a mediator with a mediation statement even in the simplest of cases.

So, how does the mediation statement affect your opening? If you've provided a statement do you need an opening? The answer in most cases is yes. Your opening is not just about apprising the mediator what your case is about. It's also about telling the other side your theory of the case. It's about letting the adjuster see you in action and feel your confidence. It's about making a connection—a connection that hopefully, will help you settle the case. If you are the plaintiff, this is the first time you have addressed the defendant directly. It may be the first time the defendant has seen your client face to face. You may want your client to say something, although I would be very careful using that tactic.

If you are the defendant, the same is true. This is your opportunity to address the plaintiff directly. Early on in this discussion, I provided an example of what a defense counsel might say to a plaintiff in a personal injury case: We recognize you were injured; we are sorry for your injuries; but we have legal defenses. That type of discussion goes beyond what the mediator needs to know but it is something the plaintiff may need to hear. To be sure, all defense attorneys do not buy into the concept that it is better to be conciliatory towards your opponent. It's not unusual to hear defense counsel spend ten minutes or so telling the plaintiff to her face that she has no case and they are here to simply offer nuisance value. That type of bluster does work but usually only when the plaintiff indeed has no case. If your ultimate goal is to settle the case, it is probably wise to temper the inflammatory remarks.

Let's spend a little more time addressing the issue of whether your client should speak during opening statement and at other times during the mediation. Once again, there is no hard and fast rule to go by. In personal injury cases, where the plaintiff is not usually that sophisticated about the legal issues, the general rule is the less said by your client, the better. Your client has already been deposed and you don't necessarily want her talking to the other side about anything that comes to her mind. It could ruin your case. On the other hand, you have the adjuster, the person who controls the purse strings, sitting at the table. Wouldn't it be a great time for that person to hear from your client how this accident has affected her? Never underestimate the power of an emotional plea. And even if that adjuster is as cold and unemotional as a block of ice, listening to your client tell her tale might make him see for the first time how effective she is going to be before a jury. Or not! And that's your decision too. She may have a great story but she may not be able to tell it very well. That would be something you wouldn't want the other side to know. Decisions, decisions.

The opposite might be true in other types of mediation, like commercial mediations where the clients are very sophisticated people. In that situation, the clients are full participants, often speaking more than the lawyers because they know the subject matter of the litigation better than the lawyers. Again, there is a lot of risk when your client talks freely in joint session and you should be very careful in making that decision and you should also know exactly what they are going to say beforehand.

Here is something that happens and that you should be prepared to deal with at any and every mediation. Say the parties have finished their openings but the mediator decides to stay in joint session and starts asking questions of the clients. This is not all that unusual. Some mediators feel that they have the authority to do this. What do you do? Remember that you are there to settle a case but if that case does not settle, the litigation is going to proceed. The Rules of Procedure require your client to sit for a deposition and answer questions. The mediator might control the process but your client is not required to answer questions in mediation, even from the mediator, and you should have no problem telling the mediator that, if she tries such a tactic. Private session is different. In private session, your client should talk openly and freely with the mediator and answer any questions the mediator asks. Why? What's the difference? The difference is that you are monitoring the conversation and you can tell the mediator at any time—"What my client just said is confidential and I don't want you conveying that information to the other side."

The mediator's job is to try and get the case settled, which necessarily means exploring what the clients' interests are. That involves asking a lot of questions. If the mediator is going to do her job effectively, the clients and the lawyers have to cooperate, and that means allowing the client in private session to speak freely with the mediator.

Stop Points

1. The mediator sets the tone for the mediation.
2. The mediator in her opening statement will advise the parties that she is only a facilitator. She is not going to decide any legal issues. Her role is to assist the parties in reaching a settlement.
3. The mediator will tell parties in her opening statements that everything said at mediation is confidential and that everything said in the private conferences is confidential.
4. You, as the lawyer, control if your client is going to speak and how much your client is going to say at mediation.
5. Normally, after the mediator's opening, both sides have the opportunity to give an opening statement.
6. After opening statements, the mediator has the option of separating the parties or keeping them in joint session.

C. Strategy

Until now, we have talked mostly about process. However, mediation is first and foremost about strategy. For the plaintiff, it is important to have a good opening statement—to inform the mediator and to let the other side know how confident you are with your position. The most important aspect of that opening, however, is the offer or demand, assuming no offers have been made up to that point. A demand is not required in opening but that's what the mediator and the defendant are looking for.

A couple of things to think about with regard to the demand: Mediation is about movement. You are going to move from your initial demand or you are not going to get your case settled. Before you ever get to the mediation table, you have to think about what your demand is going to be *and* where you want to end up. There are going to be many, many steps between that opening and where you end up and you need to put the time in and prepare a strategy and discuss that strategy with your client before you ever get to mediation. This part of your mediation strategy is almost the same as our discussion about preparation for negotiation. Your failure to discuss a strategy with your client puts you in a potential position where you are fighting with your own client and the other side. You don't have to get to the gut-wrenching stuff but you need to get your client in the ball park where you want to end up. How do you come up with your opening offer? How do you even know where the ball park is?

One thing discussed earlier about the mediator's training was the cooperative negotiating style. One of the elements of a cooperative negotiating style is the use of objective standards. What does that mean? Well, let's take some examples: if you have a personal injury case and your client has a herniated disc that has been operated on and a significant wage loss because he was a heavy laborer—you know what the elements of damages are. You can find out through jury reporters what the awards have been for these type of injuries—particularly the non-economic damages (also called "pain and suffering damages"). Then you can tailor your demand to the specific economic damages suffered by your client. If you have an employment case you can pretty much do the same thing. You know you are going to be able to get back pay and front pay for two years. Those numbers are easily calculable. You can look to other awards for non-economic damages. Divorce has different elements—child support, alimony—but the methodology is pretty much the same.

Now, let's say you do your homework and you get your number. Is that what you ask for? Maybe? The next thing you need to do is soberly and analytically look at your case. Based on the evidence what are your chances of winning? Are they 60%? 40%? 20%? If you have come up with a "number" for your damages but your analysis tells you your chances of winning are only 20% because of liability issues, for example, then you know where you want to start and where the ballpark is and where you want to walk away. Where the settlement would be worse than the alternative. In litigation, the alternative usually is the courtroom. There is no fine line to determine when the courtroom is your best alternative because you never know what a judge or a jury is going to do with your case. The best you can do is soberly analyze your case, figure out where the ball park is, and decide with your client whether the offers made by the defendant are sufficient enough for you to forego the risk of trial.

So, let's say you have analyzed your personal injury case in light of other jury awards in the area and your client's particular economic loss and you have arrived at an optimum figure of $250,000. And let's also say that through discovery you have learned about some weaknesses in your theory of liability. In your estimation you have a 40% chance of winning, and it may be as low as 20%. What do you do? The first thing you do is go over those numbers with your client. "The case would be worth $250,000 if liability was clear and you didn't have those pre-existing injuries. Because of liability problems and your prior medical history, I think the case is worth somewhere between $50,000 and $100,000." Now, hopefully, you did not oversell the value of the case to the client at the initial interview to get her business. If you did, this conversation is going to be very difficult. However, if you have provided your client with an honest assessment from the beginning—starting with that initial interview where you asked the client where you asked the client what she was looking for and gave her your initial assessment at the time—and updated that assessment as you went along, this will not be an overly difficult conversation. But if your client has had unreasonable expectations that you have not discovered and tempered, this will be a very heated discussion. Still, you need to have it *before* you walk in the door of the mediation room.

And it might not be about money. In a divorce case, it could be about custody or visitation or who gets the dog, or the toaster. In an employment case, the plaintiff may want his job back and he may forego a large monetary award. It's the mediator's role to try and find out what everybody's interests are. It's the attorney's job to determine when you want the mediator to know what you really want. Three things are necessary in mediation: patience, persistence, and timing. Have you read these words before in a previous chapter?

Getting back to the initial demand, let's take the above factual scenario as an example. What should the initial demand be? This is where the same rules from our discussion on negotiation come into play. On one hand, you don't want to make a demand that is so outrageous that it ends the mediation before it starts. On the other hand, you need room to move. Make the highest demand that you can support with reasons and give your reasons before you give your demand. If you give them the number first, they won't listen to the reasons. If you preface it, they will be anticipating the number. In the scenario above, your first demand should clearly be $250,000. You can first talk about jury awards in the local courts and you can talk about your client's particular damages. Break the number down, too. It gives it more substance—lost wages, medical bills, pain and suffering, etc. Of course, your case does not merit that amount because of liability problems, but let the defendants make that point. You've made your demand and supported it with reasons.

We have already discussed the defendant's strategy in a case of this type. Many seasoned attorneys will address the plaintiff directly, usually with several goals in mind: First, acknowledge the plaintiff's injury or loss, and second, explain to the plaintiff that the defendant has legal defenses to the claim that are not personal. The defendant might then discuss specific legal defenses and eventually, or not depending on the particular strategy, make a counteroffer. Other attorneys may choose to simply address the legal issues with the mediator and make a counteroffer or not. Still others may refuse to make any offer or acknowledge any liability.

You have to be able to react to whatever strategy is employed by opposing counsel.

Once openings are out of the way, the mediator takes over. Let's assume for the purposes of this discussion that the parties separate and go into private session right after opening statements, which is the usual case. Who does the mediator talk to first? That is up to the mediator. There is no hard and fast rule. Normally, however, the mediator will talk first to the party to whom an offer or a counteroffer has been made. For instance, if the plaintiff makes a demand but the defendant does not respond to that demand with a counteroffer, the mediator will most likely talk to the defendant. If the defendant does make a counteroffer, the mediator will most likely talk to the plaintiff.

What is that first discussion like? In most cases, the mediator will start slow with whoever she meets with. Her first goal is to make the parties feel comfortable with her. It's very much like the small talk before the negotiation begins. The mediator just wants the defendant to respond with something so the process can get started. However, if that something is insulting, the mediator may do some persuading earlier than she planned. For instance, let's say the plaintiff is a paraplegic as a result of a car accident where the defendant truck driver allegedly ran a red light and the plaintiff has a disinterested third party eyewitness to support her claim. The plaintiff's lawyer requests 2.5 million dollars in damages in his opening and breaks down the damages very specifically. Defense counsel in her opening does the "I'm sorry you were injured but we have legal defenses" routine and then proceeds to argue that there is no liability based upon her client's testimony. When the mediator meets with defense counsel in private session, counsel makes an initial offer of $5,000. (You may laugh as you read this but you would be surprised at how often this occurs.)

The mediator does not move. She talks a little bit about the weather. How she didn't have an umbrella this morning and got caught in the rain. She gets up and pours herself a cup of coffee and sits back down and eventually addresses the adjuster.

"I have no idea what you are prepared to do today but I am assuming you have a lot more money to offer than $5,000. Can you, at least, tell me that?"

"Yes."

"And am I correct in assuming that you would like to get this case resolved today?'

"Yes."

"Because you don't want to be sitting in a courtroom across from a plaintiff who is a paraplegic."

"Well, we will if we have to."

"I understand but if you had your druthers, am I correct in assuming you wouldn't want to?"

"Yes."

"Now let me ask you a question: Pretend for a moment that you are the plaintiff. You are never going to walk again. You are never going to even move your legs again. A good portion of your life has been taken from you. Are you with me?"

"Yes."

"How would you react if I, the mediator, walk back into the room where you are sitting, waiting, and tell you that the insurance company that represents the truck driver who did this to you has just offered $5,000?"

"It's just our opening offer."

"I understand, but how would you react?"

"I'd be angry."

"So angry you might just leave the mediation?"

"Maybe."

"So my question to you is—do you want to make an offer to this woman that will make her so angry she might leave the mediation?"

"No."

"Good. So maybe you and your attorney can discuss making a reasonable offer that's on the lower end of where you want to go but that you can support with reasons. I'll leave the room and let you discuss it."

The mediator is often the reality tester, as she certainly is in this situation.[7] She knows because she has seen that a $5,000 offer could cause plaintiff's coun-

---

7. There is a difference between being a tester of reality and putting undue pressure on a party to settle. Mediators certainly can and must test the parties' different positions in

sel to pack up and leave. He might not have any choice. His client might look at him and ask—"Are we going to put up with this?" He is the warrior. He has a good case. He can't let his client be insulted. A good mediator knows all this from experience.

Here is another issue that comes up in private session. Obviously, you and your client need to have a candid conversation with the mediator about what happened and what you are here for, but you may not want to tell the mediator everything. Once again, this is a matter of preference. There is no right or wrong answer. However, if you tell the mediator, for instance, in the initial private session, "if we can leave here today with a million dollars, we will be happy. But obviously I don't want them to know about that," what do you think is going to happen? The mediator can't tell the other side what your bottom line is but you have given her a blueprint and that's what she is going to shoot for. If you don't tell the mediator what your bottom line is, she has to deal with the demand that's on the table, which is a much higher figure. Now, at some point, it might be good strategy to give the mediator that bottom line figure but that should be many hours down the road when you are confident that you have bled the defendant of every dime you are going to get. Then you might want to say, "Get me this number and we will be done." There is a strategy with the mediator as well as everybody else.

Okay, back to our paraplegic case. The defendant adjuster—let's call her Theresa—after conferring with counsel, comes up with an offer of $50,000. Now the mediator, Alice, has something to work with. She can walk into the room where the plaintiff and her attorney are waiting and say, "We're making progress. It is nowhere near what you want but it is a start and it is a decent start. Let's talk a little about the liability issues. Do you know anything about this truck driver?"

"How much did they offer?"

"$50,000."

Alice is doing what you would do in a negotiation. She's selling it a little bit before she tells it. "You're going to be disappointed but it's a good start."

The job of a mediator is to ultimately get a settlement but she has to do her own fact-finding, like you did in negotiation. She has to find out what everybody's interests are so she can try to work those interests. What does that mean in a case like the one we just talked about, where everybody's interests are clearly about money? The plaintiff wants as much as she can get. The defendant wants to give as little as possible. What other issues are there? Let's see. We'll call our paraplegic plaintiff Paige.

---

light of their own experience. But mediators should never pressure any party to settle.

"Paige, what are you most afraid about in the future?" Alice, the mediator, asks.

"I don't understand?"

"Well, when you think about the future and the uncertainty of the future, what is it in particular that concerns you?"

"My medical bills. I'm going to have hundreds of thousands of dollars of medical bills. I don't have a job. I don't have insurance."

"What else?"

"I don't have a job. I can't pay my rent. I can't feed myself."

"Anything else?"

"Yes. I think I should be compensated for all I've gone through and for what my life is going to be in the future."

"Anything else?"

"Yes, my attorney needs to be paid."

"Okay. I've gone through all the numbers in your demand and from what I can tell your out of pocket bills—your lost wages, your medical bills past and future, and your attorney's fees come up to 1.5 million, is that accurate?"

"Yes."

"And your non-economic damages—what you've lost personally and permanently. You have placed a number of one million dollars on that, is that correct?"

"Yes."

"Let me ask you another question and I will keep this confidential although I may explore the issue in general with the other side depending on your answer—you were working as a secretary. Do you think that you could physically work as a secretary again?"

"Full time?"

"Yes."

"I don't know."

"Here is the big question—do you want to work?"

"Of course I want to work. I love my job but I don't want to settle this case with the idea I can work and a year down the road I can't and then I'm screwed."

"I understand. We can plan for that contingency. I just want to know if you think you can work and if you want to work."

"Like I said, I want to work but I don't know if I can."

"What did you make as a secretary?"

"Fifty thousand dollars a year. I was an executive secretary and a good one."

Alice has now gathered all the information from Paige about her hopes and fears and desires. She asks and receives permission from Paige and her lawyer, you, to discuss her working in the future as part of a settlement with the defendant. She leaves Paige and her attorney and returns to the defendant, Theresa, without a counteroffer.

"I just want to ask you some questions," Alice says to Tom.

"Okay."

"Am I correct in assuming that you want to pay as little money as possible to settle this case?"

"Of course."

"And if we can work out an arrangement that lets you pay as little as possible but compensates the plaintiff for her losses, would you be willing to do that?"

"We still have our legal defenses."

"I understand—your driver versus their independent third-party witness. Let's just for the purposes of this discussion take the liability issue off the table. Put it on the back burner, so to speak, and see if we can come up with a solution that satisfies the plaintiff's interests and your interests. Okay?"

"Okay."

"I have been talking to the plaintiff and bouncing around some ideas in my head. This doesn't come from them. It comes from me. You know this because you've done extensive discovery—this woman was an executive secretary and she was very good at her job."

"So?"

"So she might still be able to work."

"That's not what her doctor says."

"I imagine if she told her doctor she wanted to go back to work, he would allow her to try."

"What are you getting at?" Tom asks Alice.

"You're a big company. You could probably find a spot for an executive secretary. And it would probably be good for the company to have somebody with that type of disability working for you. It says something good about you. She would also qualify under your medical insurance then."

"I see what you're getting at. We can take care of the future lost wages and the future medical and get a potential good employee as well. And what happens if it doesn't work out?"

"You would have to have a contingency plan in place to cover her lost wages and medical and it would have to be a part of this agreement. She is a motivated person though. The fact that she is considering this type of arrangement is proof of that."

"Okay. Let's say we find a job for her and pay her what she made before, and give her full benefits including medical that covers her pre-existing conditions. And let's say we agree on a yearly contingency if it doesn't work out. We have those numbers, by the way. What about the rest?"

"Well, she has about eighty thousand dollars in back wages and twenty thousand in medical that her insurance didn't cover."

"Okay."

"Attorneys' fees of $400,000 on the economic damages and then we have the non-economic damages of one million."

"What do you propose?" Tom asks Alice since he has a feeling that Alice has some specific ideas.

"It's not my place to make proposals," Alice cautions. "That's for the parties to do. However, if you are asking for some input to a proposal, I would suggest that you concentrate on negotiating the non-economic damages, since they are always somewhat speculative."

"I'm not sure I want to send you in there with a proposal to put her back to work, cover all her future lost wages and medical as well as the past, and say, 'Let's talk about non-economic damages.' We'd be giving up too much." Tom says after talking to his lawyer. We have to include Tom's lawyer in here somewhere.

"I see your point," Alice says. "Why don't you make it contingent?"

"I'm not sure I know what you mean."

"Why don't you say, 'If you agree to accept X amount in non-economic damages, we will offer you a job at your old salary that would include full medical, and if that doesn't work out, we will give you X amount of dollars yearly to cover your medical insurance, deductibles, and wages, and we will pay all your outstanding past medical and past lost wages, plus an attorneys' fee of X.' That way you are not committing to anything unless they agree to your non-economic damage number."

Tom doesn't say anything for a few minutes. "I like it," he finally says. "Let me talk to my lawyer a minute." Alice leaves the room.

Tom makes a contingent offer of $300,000 in non-economic damages, which, if accepted, would trigger the rest of the deal. He further agrees to attorneys' fees of $460,000. The total up-front payout for the company including past medical and wages is $860,000, although that number could be substantially higher if the arrangement does not work out.

The negotiation continues but only on the non-economic damage issue and the attorneys' fees. Tom eventually agrees to pay $500,000 in non-economic damages but refuses to pay any more fees. The plaintiff accepts the offer.

Once an agreement is reached, it usually must be reduced to writing and signed by the parties at the mediation. The failure to have a signed agreement could kill the deal if one side decides to pull out at a later date. While the mediation is confidential, the agreement is not unless the parties agree to make it confidential.

This may not be a typical mediation, because the defendant rarely agrees to hire the plaintiff, but it could happen. It is a great example, however, of how a mediator can help the parties reach a settlement that coincides with both of their interests.

Checkpoints

- You have to have a strategy in mediation that anticipates movement. You can make an offer and stick with it, but you are probably not going to reach a settlement.

- Make the highest offer you can support with reasons.

- After opening statements, the parties usually separate in different rooms and the mediator takes over, shuttling back and forth to discuss the pros and cons of each side's case in private session.

- A good mediator starts slow, taking time to get to know the parties, but eventually, the mediator will be the tester of reality, making sure the parties don't alienate each other with bad offers and demands.

- It's the mediator's job to explore the parties' interests and try to formulate a settlement based on those interests.

- If the parties reach agreement, that agreement must be reduced to writing. While the mediation itself is confidential, the settlement agreement is not, unless the parties agree to keep it confidential.

Chapter 4

Arbitration

Roadmap

- Arbitration is the third type of alternative dispute resolution and it is the one that can most resemble a trial, although it is usually a lot less formal.

- Arbitration can be mandatory or voluntary and binding or non-binding.

- The parties to an arbitration can handle all of the administrative and planning details themselves or they can hire an administering agency/service to handle those details. This includes how many arbitrators will preside over a hearing, how those arbitrators are chosen, and what decisions those arbitrators may or must make.

- Generally, arbitration can be scheduled more quickly and be less costly than a traditional trial.

- Unless dictated by law, contract, or the administering agency/service, the parties to an arbitration can have a say on how the arbitration is to commence, how broad or restrictive discovery shall be, how quickly discovery must be completed, how disputes are to be resolved, etc.

- Generally, arbitration awards must be handed down within a specific period of time to speed up the process and are not appealable.

So now we reach the third branch of the alternative dispute resolution realm: arbitration. Simply put, arbitration is a less formal "sit-down" trial or hearing. In many ways, it looks a lot like a trial but without a judge, a jury, or the strict formalities. And since the passage of the 1925 Federal Arbitration Act, arbitration has been officially recognized as an alternative way to resolve disputes and was designed to reduce the costs and time delays of the traditional court system.[1] Like negotiation and mediation, arbitration is an adversarial process where the parties are generally opposed in their positions on the issues. And because arbitration is adversarial, having one or more arbi-

---

1. Nat'l Arbitration Forum, *Arbitration 101: The Basics of Arbitration* (2010), http://www.adrforum.com/users/naf/resources/arb%20101-21.pdf; JAY FOLBERG et al., RESOLVING DISPUTES: THEORY, PRACTICE, AND LAW 453–55 (2005).

trators preside over the hearing allows the parties to take those positions and have someone else evaluate and "judge" the appropriate outcome based on the law and facts.

For some claims or causes of action, arbitration is required to resolve the dispute. Consumer contracts, like cell phones, credit cards, or internet services contain mandatory arbitration provisions, whether the consumer knows it or not.[2] And most doctors now include an arbitration clause in their contracts with patients. Mandatory arbitration requires that the parties resolve their disputes in an arbitration hearing rather than trial. However, even if the parties did not have an arbitration clause in their initial contract to deal with future disputes, once a dispute arises, they can mutually agree in writing to submit that dispute to arbitration. And still, there are some disputes that the law requires be submitted to arbitration.[3]

But now that you know a little more about negotiation and mediation and all of their advantages, you might ask why anyone would want to engage in yet another type of dispute resolution rather than just going to trial? For those claims that require arbitration by contract, agreement, or law, that's an easy answer: they have no choice! But for those who are not required to participate in arbitration, the reasons for choosing arbitration are more numerous and varied. This portion of the text seeks to explain those reasons in two ways. Part I will review the mechanics of arbitration by detailing what arbitration is, the different forms it can take, who presides over the proceeding, what the proceedings entail, and the benefits and detriments of choosing arbitration over trial. Part II will take a look at an arbitration hearing under a microscope.

---

2. For most cell phone and credit card contracts, arbitration is mandatory for any disputes arising from either service. Most doctors now have included a mandatory arbitration clause for any payment or service disputes that arise with patients.

3. In Oregon, civil cases where the plaintiff is seeking damages of $50,000 or less, excluding attorney's fees and costs, as well as domestic relation cases are required to be submitted to arbitration for resolution. OR. REV. STAT. § 36.400 (2014). Illinois has also implemented mandatory arbitration for person injury or property damage cases where the plaintiff is seeking $30,000 or less in damages, exclusive of interests and costs. ILL. SUP. CT. RULES §§ 86–95 (2014).

I. The Mechanics of Arbitration

A. Administered versus Non-Administered/Self-Administered Arbitration

After determining whether arbitration is mandatory or voluntary, the next determination is whether the arbitration will be administered or non-administered/self-administered. Administered arbitrations are those organized and supervised by an arbitration service that takes care of matters, including vetting potential arbitrators, implementing rules regarding discovery and deadlines, scheduling the hearing, liaising between the parties and arbitrators, and all other aspects of the proceeding.[4] Non-administered/self-administered arbitrations are ones handled by the parties themselves. So which is preferable, administered or non-administered arbitrations? Well, as most things in law school, "it depends." And to better understand that, we'll look at the basic elements of arbitrations and how administered and non-administered compare as to each element, including commencing the action, the number of presiding arbitrators, choosing arbitrators, rules governing discovery and the hearing, handing down a decision, and appeals.

1. Commencing Arbitration

Once the parties decide to submit their dispute to arbitration because it is mandatory or they voluntarily choose to, they must set that plan in motion. In litigation, a claim commences when the plaintiff files a complaint and the defendant files an answer, counterclaims, and defenses with the court. In arbitration, it's similar, except the plaintiff is called the Claimant, who files a claim and the defendant is called the Respondent, who files a response, counterclaims, and defenses. But where those arbitration documents get filed may differ. In a non-administered arbitration, the parties may serve each other with these documents, because the nature of being non-administered is that the parties handle administrative matters themselves. While in administered arbitration, the parties may not only file these documents with each other, by may

---

4. Although there are local and state arbitration rules, and training/certification courses, there are three main national arbitration organizations that train/certify arbitrators and provide rules that govern the arbitration process: American Arbitration Association (AAA), International Institute for Conflict Prevention and Resolution (CPR), and Judicial Arbitration and Mediation Services, Inc., which combined with several other groups and is known as JAMS.

also file these or similar documents with the administering service according to that service's policies or procedures.[5] Or the plaintiff may file a complaint in court, but instead of filing an answer, the defendant files a Demand for Appointment of Arbitrators that lets the court know that the parties are opting for arbitration instead of trial.

The point is that the parties must file some official documents with each other, the administering service, or the court to commence arbitrating their dispute.

In addition to where these commencement documents get filed or served is what they must include. Again, this will depend on local rules or statutes, an administering service's policies, or the agreement of the parties. Typically, the Claimant's documents will include some or more of the following:

1. the pre-dispute contract provision where the parties agree to arbitration;
2. the post-dispute contract provision where the parties agree to arbitration;
3. a description of the claimant's dispute with the respondent, including any contract provision at issue;
4. description of the damages or relief sought;
5. names and contact information of the parties involved;
6. explanation or request for damages;
7. a request for a solo arbitrator or a panel of 3 arbitrators to preside; and/or
8. a fee to the administering agency.

And analogous to a defendant's answer filed in response to a complaint, the Respondent will get a chance to respond to the Claimant's documents including some or more of the following:

1. any of the Claimant's allegations;
2. any claims or defenses the Respondent may have;
3. a request that a panel of 3 arbitrators or a solo arbitrator preside; and/or

---

5. JAMS, for instance, must receive:
• a pre-dispute arbitration clause, post-dispute arbitration clause, or written confirmation of the parties' oral agreement to arbitrate that appoints JAMS as the administering agency or adopts JAMS rules to govern the arbitration; OR
• no timely objection by the Respondent as to JAMS administering the proceedings; OR
• a court's order compelling arbitration,
before it issues a Commencement Letter, which officially starts the arbitration process. JAMS COMPREHENSIVE ARBITRATION RULES AND PROCEDURES 8–9 (2014), *available at* http://www.jamsadr.com/files/Uploads/Documents/JAMS-Rules/JAMS_comprehensive_ arbitration_rules-2014.pdf (discussing Rule 5, Commencing an Arbitration) [hereinafter JAMS COMPREHENSIVE ARBITRATION].

4. a challenge to the arbitrators' jurisdiction over the matter.

Generally, the purpose of these initial claim documents is to put all parties on notice of the nature of the dispute, the parties involved, any counterclaims or defenses, the relief sought, and how many arbitrators will preside. This helps get all parties on the same page before moving forward. And because getting into the details of any and all the claims and counterclaims that are case specific and therefore far too numerous to get into here, the next matter we'll address is the number of arbitrators to preside over a hearing and how those arbitrators are chosen.

2. Number of Arbitrators and How Chosen

An arbitrator is a neutral third party who assists parties to resolve their claims. Arbitrators, sometimes referred to as neutrals, are similar to mediators in that they are neutral in the matter, but different in that they engage in a more active "judge-like" role. Arbitrators preside over scheduling matters before the arbitration hearing, set deadlines for discovery and motions, resolve discovery or motion disputes, preside over the arbitration hearing, decide evidentiary and witness matters, render a decision in the case, and assess remedies, if appropriate.

In arbitration, either a solo arbitrator presides over the hearing or a panel of three do. Each has its pros and cons and considering those, can help the parties decide. First, a solo arbitrator is usually easier to schedule conferences with and contact by phone to resolve matters because you're only dealing with one person. However, if that solo arbitrator is just not sympathetic to your client's position, there is no one else to try to win over to gain support for your client. On the flip side, trying to schedule hearings with 3 arbitrators or getting all 3 to agree on a matter may be more challenging because 3 people means 3 different calendars, personalities, and perspectives. However, if one of the 3 arbitrators does not sympathize with your client's position, the other 2 may, and so your client still has a chance to prevail. Two out of three is better than none out of one. Second, consider the cost involved. Because each arbitrator gets a fee for their services, having one arbitrator preside costs less than having a panel of three. Third, consider how simple or complex the issues involved in the dispute are. If it's a straightforward breach of contract or a property damage claim, one arbitrator may be sufficient. However, the more complex the issues are, the more arbitrators you may want to help appreciate the nuances of those issues. And a fourth consideration is how the arbitrators are to be chosen and appointed. Whether the parties have a say in choosing the arbitrators or whether the court or administering services chooses can impact the outcome of the claim. Those wanting more of a say in who presides would probably want a panel of three where they can choose at least one of the three, the opponent may choose one, and those two arbitrators would choose the third. That way, each party has someone on the panel they believe is on their side with a neutral breaking the tie. For those who don't want to choose or have the other side choose, having just one arbitrator may be preferable by letting the court or administering agency appoint that one arbitrator.

And although there may be other considerations, the four listed above cover the most common ones. Now, some administering services suggest just one arbitrator preside unless the parties agree otherwise to a panel of three.[6] Therefore, those services suggest that one arbitrator is usually enough. However, the parties can veer from that suggestion and choose a panel of three if they want. Again, unless it's required in the parties' contract, agreement, or the law, the parties can choose one or three arbitrators based on some of the pros and cons discussed—quick scheduling, complexity of the issues involved, costs, and wanting a say in who presides or not.

Although touched on above, the next step is how those arbitrators are chosen and appointed to preside once the parties agree on a number. If using an administering agency, their rules contain intricate formulas for how this occurs. So, for instance, if only one arbitrator will preside over a claim for $75,000 or less, the agency will choose that arbitrator from its list of certified arbitrators, without the parties' input.[7] Or, for claims over $75,000, the agency will provide both parties with an identical list of 5 potential arbitrators, allow the parties a period of time in which to strike 2 names from the list, and then the agency will appoint one of the remaining names. However, if for some reason no name can be chosen from that list, the agency may choose another name not on that list without having to send the parties a new list. And if some of these rules sound complicated, they are! And if you can believe it, the rules for how to choose a panel of three arbitrators are even more complex! But again, the administering agencies have considered many scenarios that parties face when choosing arbitrators, and drafted rules to deal with each contingency. Therefore, if the parties face one of these scenarios, instead of stopping the arbitration in its tracks, the parties just look for the rule that explains what

---

6. American Arbitration Association [AAA], *Non-Binding Arbitration Rules for Consumer Disputes and Business Disputes* 6 (2009) (discussing Rule 10. PDF-file is available on the AAA website, https://www.adr.org, under "Rules & Procedures," and "Rules."); JAMS Comprehensive Arbitration, *supra* note 4, at 11 (discussing Rule 7, Number and Neutrality of Arbitrators; Appointment and Authority of Chairperson).

7. AAA, *supra* note 7, at 5 (discussing Rule 9(a)).

to do next. And another benefit of using an administering agency is that if the parties have a question as to the proper interpretation or application of a rule, the agency will act to clarify it to allow the proceedings to go forward.

However, even if the parties do not choose to use the administering agency to organize and run the arbitration, the parties can "adopt" an agency's rules for the purpose of governing the arbitration, the parties can draft their own rules and method for choosing the arbitrators, or they can create a hybrid of the two. And if the parties must participate in arbitration under law, then, some courts have their own rules for choosing arbitrators. So non-administered arbitration does not mean that the parties must figure everything out on their own in terms of every possible contingency, because they can use the agency's rules, but the parties don't get the benefit of having the agency there to help resolve any problems with rule interpretation or application.

3. *Who Can Be an Arbitrator and How To Choose the Best Arbitrators*

So after determining how many arbitrators will preside and who can choose them, the next questions have to be who can actually be an arbitrator and if a party can be involved in the process of choosing one, how should the party go about doing that?

First, like mediators, there is usually some degree of training or experience required to become an arbitrator. Although each state has different requirements, generally arbitrators are attorneys or law school graduates, while less often, they are those with any college degree.[8] Most states or administering agencies require arbitrators to participate in some approved training courses, shadow or attend a certain number of arbitrations, and/or complete a test or exercise to become certified. Once certified, arbitrators are usually added to a list of certified arbitrators with a designation of any legal specialty they may have.

If arbitrators are trained by an administering service (like AAA, JAMS, CPR), that agency will place them on its list of certified arbitrators. Parties using that administering service would then have access to those arbitrators who are specifically trained by those agencies and familiar with their rules and procedures. For those trained by other services, their names might end up on a court-approved list of arbitrators or state or local bar association list as qualified arbitrators.

However, it is less common for jurisdictions to not require any special training or certification to become an arbitrator, and therefore it is equally less com-

---

8. Finra, *Arbitration & Mediation, Become an Arbitrator,* http://www.finra.org/ArbitrationAndMediation/Arbitrators/BecomeanArbitrator/ (last visited Aug. 11, 2014).

mon for attorneys to want to hire an untrained arbitrator to preside. Which brings us to the question of if parties have the option to help choose arbitrators, how should they go about doing that?

As discussed earlier, sometimes local rules or the contract the parties signed govern who and how the arbitrators are chosen and if so, then those rules must be followed. However, if it's the parties' choice, then there are many ways in which the arbitrators are chosen. It can be common for the attorneys for both sides to work together to choose the arbitrator(s). In some cases, each attorney will submit the name of one arbitrator and those two arbitrators will choose the third. This gives each side some, but not complete, control over who'll preside. And having the two chosen arbitrators pick the third arbitrator ensures a level of fairness with neither party having the majority of panel members siding with one side. Other times, the attorneys may each draft a list of 3–5 approved arbitrators and share their lists with opposing counsel to see if there are any agreed-upon names. Other times, one party may not have a preference and may allow the other side to choose an arbitrator or arbitrators off of a court- state- or national-approved list. Last, sometimes the court or clerk chooses the arbitrator(s).

When there is a choice involved, the parties should take an active role in appointing who presides. So just like when choosing a mediator, attorneys may choose arbitrators based on their knowledge of the specific legal area in dispute. Therefore, an attorney who specializes in construction law may be an arbitrator who presides over construction law cases because she is well versed in the subject area. However, her expertise does not limit her from only presiding over construction law cases because, as an attorney, she is qualified to be involved with any legal issue. But when attorneys are trying to resolve a case involving a specialized legal area through arbitration, they are more apt to seek out arbitrators familiar with that legal area.

Now, as also discussed in the mediation section, just because the arbitrator has expertise in that specific area of law does not mean that the arbitration will run flawlessly, but it is probably beneficial that the arbitrator understands some of the complexities and nuances of the matter. And the same is true that attorneys representing clients with more general claims may have less of a preference on an arbitrator's area of expertise and would be satisfied simply with an arbitrator's years of experience presiding over arbitration hearings. Regardless of whether you seek an arbitrator with a specific or general area of expertise, when choosing arbitrators, check their qualifications carefully. Consider whether an arbitrator tends to preside over certain types of claims, is hired by certain clients repeatedly, or tends to favor certain parties. For instance, earlier in the mediation chapter, we met Norman, with a retaliation claim against his large corporate employer. Let's say that both sides agree to arbitrate the claim and as Norman's lawyer, you identify a possible arbitrator who was an employment law attorney for 20 years. At first glance, the arbitrator may seem well suited to preside over the hearing because of her knowledge of employment law. However, after more careful research, you realize that for the last 18 years of her legal practice, the arbitrator defended employers and management. So although she is knowledgeable, she may not be as sympathetic to Norman's claim because she relates more to the employer's position. Now of course, the presumption is that any arbitrator should be impartial when presiding over a hearing. But let's be honest, people are people, and if someone has spent 18 years with the perspective that employers and companies have been unfairly taken advantage of by unhappy employees who sue, or that courts tend to favor employees in their rulings, that attorney-turned-arbitrator will consciously or not, tend to want to right the wrongs she has witnessed over the years by siding more with employers and management. That is not to say that every or even many arbitrators would draft patently or latently biased opinions, but it's important to consider how human nature plays a role in every proceeding, legal or not. It's analogous to the discussion in the negotiation section about how emotions are both present and unpredictable in every situation because that's human nature.

Another consideration when choosing arbitrators is whether they are chosen or appointed repeatedly by the same companies or clients. Consider a credit card company going to arbitration repeatedly to resolve disputes with consumers about late payments or changes in the annual percentage rate. That credit card company's arbitration clause may require that all arbitrations take place in a certain jurisdiction chosen by the company, let's say in Pennsylvania. If all of the credit card company's arbitrations will take place in Pennsylvania, the company would probably end up using the same or many of the same arbitrators each time. If that credit card company generates a substantial portion of the arbitrators' business, there is a chance that the arbitrators will tend to issue opinions favorable to the credit card company to secure repeat business. The phrase "Don't bite the hand that feeds you" comes to mind. Again, this is not to say that these arbitrators would not be ethical or professional, but there is the human element of wanting to stay in business and continually ruling against one of your biggest clients is probably not the best way to keep that client's business.

So when scrutinizing the arbitrators' qualifications, you need to carefully identify some of these possible biases or tendencies. Because of the potential for bias, having a three-person arbitration panel may be the most neutral solution, where the parties mutually agree to two arbitrators and those two arbitrators choose the third. Therefore, no one side has the balance of power on the panel. Another option, which has been adopted by some administering services and courts, is that if each party is to appoint an arbitrator to a three-person panel, that arbitrator must be completely neutral to that party. That means that the arbitrator cannot have a bias towards the party appointing him/her. And there may be some degree of proof or statement made by the arbitrator to that effect so that it is clear that the arbitrator will not favor the appointing party during the proceedings.

And even though there are no guarantees of a "perfect" arbitration, considering the best type of arbitrator for the particular claim and choosing that arbitrator may have a beneficial outcome on the proceeding. It's similar to deciding who would make the best juror for a trial. It's an art, not a science, but attorneys use experts, their own experience, the facts of the case, the likability of the client and witnesses, the complexity of the issues, and many other criteria to determine who would be the most sympathetic jurors to decide the client's case favorably. Although lawyers can calculate the variables and create mathematical equations to predict what makes a favorable juror, there is one completely unpredictable criteria—human nature. People may not always act as you think they should, might, or have in the past and it's no different when choosing an arbitrator. But regardless of the "unpredictability," it's still smarter for attorneys to take an active role in considering who would make the best arbitrator(s) for their client's case.

Here's where the administering agencies can help when choosing arbitrators. Most of these agencies vet or screen their arbitrators to identify any potential conflicts or bias towards or against a party involved. Some agencies will allow each party to choose an arbitrator and then the agency will query those choices to disclose any reasons why they might be perceived as unable to be independent or impartial. The agency would then circulate that information to the parties to give them a certain amount of time in which to object. The agency would then take the objection under consideration and allow the non-objecting party to respond. If no response is received or the agency overrules the objection, then the "challenged" arbitrator will be appointed.[9] If the agency sustains the objection, then another process is put into place to appoint a non-challenged arbitrator. Again, this is where some of the agency rules can get a little specific if not even a little complicated. But that is one of the benefits of hiring an administering agency to handle all of these intricacies if, or when, they arise. They have dealt with many of these issues before and can handle these

---

9. Conflict Prevention & Resolution (CPR) Procedures & Clauses Administered Arbitration Rules 8–9 (2013) (discussing Rule 5.1(c)) [hereinafter CPR Rules].

matters so that the parties do not need to resolve any more conflicts other than the claims relevant to the arbitration proceeding itself. Not surprisingly, because arbitration is an adversarial process, even small bumps in the road can create unnecessary stress or roadblocks to the parties resolving the "big" issues. An administering agency can calm a potentially tense situation by resolving it so the parties can direct their time and attention elsewhere and not at blaming each other for slowing down the process or throwing a wrench in the machine. And other times, when the parties want to be involved in resolving even these minor issues, the administering agency can act as a referee of sorts to keep the parties focused, calm, and moving forward.

Another consideration is the arbitrator's availability. If the parties agree on an arbitrator who is not available for at least six months, they may choose another arbitrator so that the case can proceed more quickly. Again, one of the benefits of arbitration is not being subject to the court's busy calendar, but instead working around the parties' and arbitrators' calendars. Although in litigation, the parties generally do not have the option to choose a different judge with a lighter calendar, parties agreeing to arbitrate can choose other arbitrators based on their preferences and schedules.

Here again is where administering agencies come into play. In addition to vetting potential arbitrators for any potential biases, the agency can also determine the arbitrators' availability and pass that information along to the parties. This can help the process of choosing arbitrators to go even more quickly so the parties know very early on whether an arbitrator would even be available when needed.

Another consideration is the location of the arbitration. Some arbitrators have office space to accommodate the arbitration hearings or have agreements with businesses to use their facilities for hearings, which again may factor into being chosen by parties. For example, one party may want the "courtroom" feel because it is more akin to a trial, or the nature of the case requires more of a courtroom setup and therefore a larger space is necessary. Others may only be interested in having a space available quickly so that the hearing can proceed sooner rather than later.

It is customary to pay for use of this space either as part of or separate from the administering agency's fee, or a fee that parties would pay directly to the owner of the space. As part of using an administering agency, many of the costs would be listed right up front so the parties would know with some degree of certainty how much the arbitration process would cost. However, for those choosing not to use an administering agency, some of these costs may not be something that the parties have considered and therefore may come as more of a shock. So regardless to whom the fee is paid, location cost is another concern for parties when deciding to arbitrate rather than litigate, as parties do not pay the court to use the courthouse to try a case.

Stop Points

1. The parties to a dispute need to know whether arbitration is mandatory (pursuant to contract, statute, or law) or voluntary. If mandatory, then the parties must resolve their dispute through arbitration; if voluntary, the parties can choose to resolve the dispute through arbitration.
2. Once the parties decide arbitration is how their dispute is to be resolved, they must decide whether they will hire an administering agency or service to organize and supervise the proceedings, or whether they will conduct a non-administered/self-administered proceeding.
3. Commencing the arbitration is the next step, which usually requires documents filed first by the claimant, describing the claims being brought against whom, and then by the respondent, responding to those claims and raising any counterclaims or defenses. Those documents are then usually served on the opposing party, with the court, and/or with the administering agency along with a filing fee.
4. The parties must then decide whether one or three arbitrators will preside over the proceedings and how those arbitrators are chosen. The decision may be part of the parties' contract, decided by the administering agency, by law, or the parties' agreement.
5. Usually arbitrators must be lawyers or law school graduates who have gone through some training and certification to be an arbitrator. Once certified, their names are placed on state-approved lists or within an administering agency's roster. If an arbitrator has an expertise in a specialized area, that may be noted as well on these lists or rosters.
6. If the parties have some say in who is an arbitrator, they should take an active role. They should carefully scrutinize arbitrators' backgrounds, experience, hiring history, etc., to help determine any biases they may have. Administering agencies will help vet the arbitrators' potential conflicts.

4. *Rules Governing Arbitration and the Discovery Process*

So like all legal proceedings, there are rules that govern arbitrations and arbitrators. Your jurisdiction, the entity that certified the arbitrator(s), or even the contract or arbitration agreement between the parties may have clear rules that must be followed during arbitrations. Those rules may guide some of the matters we've already addressed like the number of arbitrators who shall preside and how those arbitrators are chosen and appointed. However, rules also govern many other issues, like how soon an arbitration hearing must take place once the arbitration process is commenced, whether the arbitration will be binding or non-binding, what the discovery process can or must entail, and whether the arbitration proceeding will be in-person or by telephone/virtual attendance. So let's address each in turn.

5. Time Frames for Arbitration

Because one of the primary benefits of arbitration is that it is a legal process that can resolve disputes more quickly than litigation, most court rules and administering agency rules require that once the arbitration process is commenced, it be completed expeditiously. For instance, in Cook County, Illinois, an arbitration hearing must be held within 1 year from commencement, unless the court extends that time for good cause.[10] Or under AAA's streamlined

---

10. Rule 88, of the Illinois Supreme Court Rules, Scheduling of Hearing, states,

The procedure for fixing the date, time and place of a hearing before a panel of arbitrators shall be prescribed by circuit rule provided that not less than 60 days' notice in writing shall be given to the parties or their attorneys of record. The hearing shall be held on the scheduled date and within one year of the date of filing of the action, unless continued by the court upon good cause shown. The hearing shall be held at a location provided or authorized by the court.

This rule was adopted in May 20, 1987 and went into effective June 1, 1987. And additionally, for court appointed/mandatory arbitration, the court system may act as the administering agency, according to Rule 18.1 Administration of Mandatory Arbitration of the State of Illinois Circuit Court of Cook County,

(a) The Chief Judge shall appoint a Supervising Judge for Arbitration in each Municipal District, who shall have the powers and responsibilities set forth in these rules and who shall serve at the pleasure of the Chief Judge.

(b) The Chief Judge shall appoint an Arbitration Administrator who shall have the authority and responsibilities set forth in these rules, and who shall serve at the pleasure of the Chief Judge.

(c) Clerical and support staff necessary for the effective administration of the arbitration program shall be appointed by the Chief Judge. The number of clerical and support personnel, and the compensation paid to such employees, shall be approved by the Supreme Court.

(d) Clerical and support personnel shall serve at the pleasure of the Chief Judge and may be removed by the Chief Judge.

(e) The amount of compensation to be paid any Arbitration Administrator or clerical and support personnel shall be paid by the State.

(f) No administrative, clerical or support personnel receiving compensation from any public funds under the provisions of these rules shall receive any compensation, gift, or gratuity whatsoever from any person, firm, or corporation for doing or refraining from

schedule, unless the parties agree otherwise, the entire arbitration process should not exceed 120 days (6 months) from commencement.[11] And these are just two examples representative of the desire courts, agencies, and parties have to keep arbitrations timely. And as a reminder, except for criminal cases that constitutionally require that defendants receive a speedy trial,[12] civil cases do not have that same right and therefore can take much longer to go to trial than 6 months to a year. In fact, depending on how complicated the case is or how backlogged the court calendar is, it can take several years to even get a trial date scheduled from the time the complaint is filed.

6. Binding v. Non-Binding Arbitration and Finality of Awards

Arbitrations can be binding, where the parties agree that whatever result the arbitrators reach, the parties accept to resolve their dispute. Arbitrations can also be non-binding, where the parties receive what's akin to an "advisory" ruling of how their claim would resolve. Not surprisingly, sometimes the parties' contract, agreement, or the law dictate whether the parties can or must participate in binding or non-binding arbitration. And, also not surprisingly, there are pros and cons to both, so let's discuss those and the details of each type of arbitration, starting with binding arbitration.

Binding arbitration is exactly what it says—the decision handed down by the solo arbitrator or panel of arbitrators will resolve the parties' dispute with finality. The most obvious benefit is that the claim is over and not subject to numerous appeals. It's not uncommon for the public to get frustrated with the legal system because of what seems like the lack of finality in cases that go on for years after the conclusion of trial because the parties get wrapped up in appeals. Lawyers and judges know that the appellate process is in place to protect the rights of the parties involved and to ensure the integrity of the legal system. However, outsiders do not always appreciate those protections and for the parties involved, the length of time to "finalize" a verdict can seem to take longer than necessary. In fact, final arbitration awards are only subject to being vacated or appealed under very limited circumstances, such as where one or more parties procured the arbitration award by "corruption, fraud, or undue means" or where one or more arbitrators were corrupt or too biased towards

---

doing any official act in any way connected with any proceeding then pending or yet to be instituted before any court or arbitration panel. Violation of this rule shall be grounds for immediate termination.

This rule was amended July 30, 2001, and took effect August 1, 2001.

11. AAA, *supra* note 8, at 2 (providing a Streamlined Schedule).

12. U.S. Const. amend. XI.

or against a party.[13] Parties wanting to resolve their dispute more quickly and definitively may give up those protections afforded in a trial and the appellate process by choosing binding arbitration.

Non-binding arbitrations are again, exactly what they seem — arbitrations that issue an award/opinion that is only advisory to the parties. You may be asking why anyone would want to go through the arbitration process, which in some ways can be complicated, only to receive an opinion that is not binding on either party, and does not resolve the dispute? Well, in Florida, for instance, there is an arbitration initiative aptly named Arbitration Florida that is designed to encourage parties involved in a medical malpractice action to participate in arbitration and allows judges to submit the case to non-binding arbitration.[14] But why would states do that? Generally, it's to get the parties to take a hard and honest look at what may happen at trial where it will take longer to schedule, cost a lot more to put on a case, and include the uncertainty of what a jury might decide. By having an arbitration panel hand down a decision, it may make the parties think about whether settling or binding arbitration may be the way to go. Also, if the parties are satisfied with the non-binding decision, they can agree to abide by it and therefore make the non-binding arbitration binding by agreement after the fact.[15]

---

13. Federal Arbitration Act, 9 U.S.C. § 10 (2012) states,

(a) In any of the following cases the United States court in and for the district wherein the award was made may make an order vacating the award upon the application of any party to the arbitration —

(1) where the award was procured by corruption, fraud, or undue means;

(2) where there was evident partiality or corruption in the arbitrators, or either of them;

(3) where the arbitrators were guilty of misconduct in refusing to postpone the hearing, upon sufficient cause shown, or in refusing to hear evidence pertinent and material to the controversy; or of any other misbehavior by which the rights of any party have been prejudiced; or

(4) where the arbitrators exceeded their powers, or so imperfectly executed them that a mutual, final, and definite award upon the subject matter submitted was not made.

(b) If an award is vacated and the time within which the agreement required the award to be made has not expired, the court may, in its discretion, direct a rehearing by the arbitrators.

(c) The United States district court for the district wherein an award was made that was issued pursuant to section 580 of title 5 may make an order vacating the award upon the application of a person, other than a party to the arbitration, who is adversely affected or aggrieved by the award, if the use of arbitration or the award is clearly inconsistent with the factors set forth in section 572 of title 5.

14. Fla. Stat. Ann. § 766.107 (West 1997 & Supp. 1998).

15. And parties in any non-binding arbitration may agree to accept the advisory opinion as binding, not just those arbitrations contemplated by Florida's Arbitration Initiative

And Florida goes even further than court-ordered non-binding arbitration, by encouraging parties to a medical malpractice claim to engage in voluntary binding arbitration as to damages only if the defendant is willing to admit liability.[16] Why would the defendant want to admit liability or why would the defendant's attorney allow the defendant to admit liability when it seems to go against everything we've been taught about making "admissions" in a legal context? Well, by admitting liability and arbitrating damages only, the defendant limits the damages the plaintiff can be awarded. For example, the arbitrators cannot award punitive damages to the plaintiff, the plaintiff's non-economic damages (or damages for pain and suffering, loss of enjoyment of life, etc. or what are considered the "intangible" damages) are capped at $250,000, and the plaintiff's wage loss and loss of earning capacity are limited to 80%. Additionally, the defendant's admission of liability cannot be used against her in future claims or even for this claim.

So now you might be asking, with all these limitations on the plaintiff's recovery, why would a plaintiff want to agree to binding arbitration in a medical malpractice claim? First, it makes the plaintiff's side easier to not have to prove both liability and damages, so it reduces the costs and fees that the plaintiff has to pay his attorney.

Second, it still allows for a significant amount of damages, and although the plaintiff is not guaranteed the highest amount of damages, unless the plaintiff cannot show any damages, the plaintiff is guaranteed to be awarded some damages. The same is not true at trial, where the jury can be very unpredictable. In fact, it is possible for a plaintiff to not only lose at trial, with the jury returning a verdict for the defendant, but the plaintiff could also be held responsible to pay the defendant's attorney's fees and costs![17]

Third, the defendant is responsible to pay the plaintiff's reasonable attorney's fees and costs.

Fourth, and this can be both a pro and con, by opting for arbitration, the plaintiff agrees to forgo any other legal avenue against the defendant for this claim. So yes, the plaintiff is giving up his right to a trial and appeals, but the plaintiff is also getting a quicker and somewhat more certain resolution. And for many injured plaintiffs, some money now is better than the mere potential of more money later.

---

in medical malpractice cases. Stephen C. Bennett *Non-Binding Arbitration: An Introduction*, 61 Disp. Res. J., May–July 2006, at 1, 3.

16. Remember that medical malpractice is a tort of negligence, which requires the plaintiff to prove liability and damages. Fla. Stat. §766.203 (2014).

17. Fla. Stat. §768.79 (2014); Fla. R. Civ. Pro. §1.442.

So again, another big question that parties need to ask themselves is whether they want the arbitration to be binding and therefore final, for all intents and purposes, or non-binding and advisory.

Stop Points

1. One benefit to resolving a dispute through arbitration is that you can schedule an arbitration hearing much sooner than a trial. Many administering agency rules require that an arbitration be resolved within so many days or months from commencement.
2. If not governed by contract, rule, or statute, the parties may be able to decide whether they want the arbitration to be binding and therefore final as to the dispute, or non-binding and therefore more of an advisory opinion.
3. Even if a non-binding decision is handed down by the arbitrators, the parties can agree to its terms and make it binding.
4. Binding arbitration awards are final and may only be vacated or appealed on very limited grounds, such as an award being procured by a party's fraud or an arbitrator's corruption.

7. Discovery

But whether the matter will be handled by one or more arbitrators, be binding or non-binding, or organized by an administering agency or self-administered, the parties may engage in some degree of discovery before an arbitration hearing. The discovery process, or the process of exchanging information and documents about the case with all parties, is also what happens to parties who go to trial rather than arbitration. And invariably, the parties will have disagreements about discovery requests such as what the request should include or be limited to, what format the response should take, and how detailed an e-discovery request must be. So let's examine what the discovery process looks like in arbitration and how discovery disputes are generally handled.

a. The Arbitration Discovery Process

In litigation, the Federal or State Rules of Civil Procedure govern discovery and other procedural matters to ensure fairness and provide structure by requiring all parties to act in good faith and allow each side to "discover" relevant information, documents, evidence, testimony, test results, etc., to assist in supporting or defending the claims at issue.[18] The rules dictate what types of information, documents, evidence, testimony, test results, etc., can be requested; how they can be requested; how often they can be requested; and what must be produced and when to the requesting party or parties. The idea is not to have a "smoking gun" appear at the "eleventh hour" during trial. Discovery acts to "level the playing field" so that all parties are privy to the same documents, information, witnesses, evidence, and law. So although movies and television shows create drama when one party has information that was not shared with the other party, but should have been shared, or one party learns information at the very last second before the jury's verdict is read, those situations rarely occur and discovery helps to prevent them.

Additionally, in litigation, the Federal or State Rules of Evidence govern what information obtained during discovery can actually be used to support a claim or defense, or can be admitted during trial. Just like the Civil Procedure Rules, the Rules of Evidence are designed to ensure that only the most credible evidence is used at trial so that the parties are properly supporting their side of the case, allowing the opposing party the opportunity to test or query the evidence for holes or weaknesses, and not misleading the jury and judge. As each question is asked of a witness on direct or cross-examination or each document is presented to the jury, the parties and judge are scrutinizing whether the questions, answers, or documents meet these high evidentiary standards. As to arbitration, the only hard and fast Federal Rule of Evidence that applies is to protect information and documents protected by privilege or work product.[19]

The arbitrator(s) help guide the parties through the discovery process just like a judge, to make sure that information is timely and accurately shared among parties. So just like you wouldn't go to trial without having investigated your client's claim, your opponent's defenses, and the law, you wouldn't go to an arbitration without doing the same. Therefore, parties are expected to have "done their homework" beforehand so that the arbitration hearing itself is the culmination of the parties' discovery, negotiations, and failure to resolve the matter themselves.

Although the parties to arbitration are also expected to act in good faith when they engage in discovery, and that discovery must have some relevance

---

18. *See generally* Fed. R. Civ. Pro. 1.
19. JAMS Comprehensive Arbitration, *supra* note 4, at 24 (discussing Rule 22(d)).

to the claims, counterclaims, and defenses raised, because arbitration is not as formal as a trial, generally the length of time for discovery is shorter, the depth of discovery shallower, and the rules of evidence either act as a guide or do not apply at all. But let's start with the discovery process first.

One of the most expensive and expansive areas of arbitration and litigation is discovery, and yet it's the end product of that discovery process that serves as a party's support for its claims or defenses. Now, as discussed above, one of the main benefits of choosing arbitration over trial is how much more quickly the parties can schedule a date for, prepare for, and participate in an arbitration hearing. However, those good intentions were not always abided by. As arbitration became more popular and accessible during the 1980s and 1990s, especially as to complex litigation cases, attorneys made the arbitration process more complex as well, almost mimicking the formal requirements of trial. Attorneys expanded discovery to become too broad, filed more dispositive motions, applied the Federal Rules of Evidence too strictly, and even requested review of arbitration[20] awards and opinions too often.[21] These attorney-driven changes to arbitration resulted in the Uniform Arbitration Act being significantly revised in 2000, which implemented many changes to the arbitration process.[22] However, all these changes and additions to the arbitration process even further eroded some of the main benefits of arbitration including speed, ease, and lower costs.

During the past 5 years, parties have responded to the U.A.A.'s 2000 revisions by more readily agreeing to a scaled down version of discovery so that arbitration remains a truly attractive alternative to litigation.[23] For example, JAMS offers Expedited Procedures established in 2010 to condense the discovery process by allowing each side to depose only one person—the opponent or someone within the opponent's control.[24] If a party needs an additional deposition, it is within the arbitrator's discretion to determine whether that party has the appropriate need for the additional deposition and whether there is a less burdensome discovery method available. Additionally, JAMS limits the production of hard copy and e-documents to only those that are relevant, non-privileged, within the party's control, and support that party's position.[25] Lastly,

---

20. Dispute Resolution and e-Discovery § 10:1 (database updated Dec. 2013) by Richard Chemick & Carl J. West, JAMS and E-Discovery § 10:1.
21. *Id.*
22. Id.
23. JAMS Comprehensive Arbitration, *supra* note 4, at 21 (discussing Rule 17(a)).
24. *Id.*
25. *Id.*

JAMS requires that the documents be exchanged with the opponents within 21 days after the filing of all arbitration pleadings and claims.[26]

AAA also has a similar streamlined discovery process with the same purpose[27]: to limit the scope, depth, and length of time for discovery to move the process along as quickly and efficiently as possible.

However, parties are not limited to the streamlined clauses just discussed, and may include more expansive discovery clauses in their arbitration agreements, but such clauses are disfavored if they are too broad and all-encompassing.[28] So for instance, a clause that provides for "discovery consistent with the Federal Rules of Civil Procedure," or "any and all documents directly or indirectly related to matter X," would be proper in scope for trial, but not arbitration.[29] To prepare for trial, it makes sense that the parties would want to cast a wider discovery net to anticipate issues and matters that "may" arise. However, because arbitration aims to be more focused and efficient, the parties are encouraged to pare down the disputed issues and tailor their discovery only to those issues. And keeping discovery tied to the actual issues, claims, and defenses allows for a more focused arbitration hearing. Instead, arbitration discovery should be proportionate to the amount in dispute, the case's complexity, and the actual need for the information to be exchanged.[30] Any more specific provisions are disfavored because they tend to permit discovery that is far too broad in time and scope before the issues have been pared down. At the beginning of an arbitration claim, it's not uncommon for the parties to want to be more inclusive with discovery. But allowing discovery in arbitration to equal that in a civil action can be dangerous because it is too all-encompassing and may not be able to be properly limited by the arbitrators.

This is best exemplified by e-discovery, which is becoming more prevalent in all claims, even those considered commonplace or simple. E-discovery is electronically stored information and documents.[31] So many law firms and companies are going paperless, which means that their only copy of documents is electronically stored. But it's not only documents that are more often stored electronically—people communicate a lot more electronically than ever

26. *Id.*

27. AAA, *supra* note 8, at 1 (discussing the Streamlined Process).

28. *Id.* at 7 (providing Rule 15(a), which states that "Depositions, interrogatories, and requests to admit, as developed in American court procedures, are not appropriate procedures for obtaining information in non-binding arbitration").

29. JAMS Comprehensive Arbitration, *supra* note 8, at 19–21 (discussing Rule 16.2).

30. *Id.*

31. *Supra.*

before. So requesting e-mails, texts, or even phone call logs requires accessing electronically stored information. And then within the electronic format is information called "metadata," which provides additional levels of detail about the document's creation date, including any date it was changed or altered and any time it was deleted (or attempted to be deleted). This metadata may include information that a normal hard copy document would not have and that therefore one party may not want the other party to obtain. Or one party may specifically request the metadata of a particular document.

So to tailor e-discovery to what is more reasonable, the parties are urged to limit e-discovery to those electronic sources and media that are used in the ordinary course of a party's business that the party would have relatively easy access to, and not to any back-up servers or other non-searchable media storage systems.

Also, whether computer experts may need to be hired or consulted to either retrieve such information or protect and redact such information from being discovered by the opposing party is yet another factor that will impact the time and cost involved in e-discovery. Therefore, arbitrators may deny or limit e-discovery requests that are too costly or burdensome for the type of dispute or amount in controversy.[32]

Arbitration discovery is intended to be more limited in scope, depth, response time, and cost to alleviate the burdens on both the requesting and responding parties.

The discovery rules that apply to arbitration whether created by statutes, administering services, or the parties themselves do and should further those purposes.

b. Preventing and Resolving Arbitration Discovery Disputes

We know that parties to an arbitration may agree to use an administering agency's discovery rules, draft their own, or use some hybrid; however, disputes will still arise about the discovery process that must be resolved. So what happens if the parties agree to limited and expedited discovery but then they disagree on how to resolve an issue that arises about discovery? Maybe one party thinks the discovery request is too broad, too cumbersome, too expensive, or delves into confidential matters. Who decides what to do next? The arbitrators do, usually with a preliminary or prehearing conference and then, if necessary, with other conferences as additional issues arise. So let's address the preliminary or prehearing conference first.

---

32. JAMS Comprehensive Arbitration, *supra* note 4, at 20 (discussing Rule 16.2(c)(iv)).

In litigation, parties attend scheduling or pretrial conferences to make sure that the parties agree to when the trial will be scheduled, time frames for when discovery should be completed, deadlines for motions, etc. And parties are not limited to one such conference, especially in more complex cases with multiple parties, experts, and massive discovery. Arbitration is similar in that the parties can either request such a conference or if they choose to adopt an administering agency's rules, most agency rules require such a conference. And similar to litigation, these conferences may cover such matters as discovery deadlines, any agreement of the parties to narrow or clarify the issues, any agreement to change the arbitration hearing structure, setting a deadline for the exchange of witness names who will testify at the hearing, scheduling any dispositive motions, pre-marking exhibits, preparing joint exhibit lists, pre-determining the admissibility of any exhibits, determining the form the award will take, and any other matters deemed necessary by the parties.[33] Some agencies will allow this conference to be attended by phone or in person, and for additional conferences to be held as needed, perhaps once the discovery process is complete.[34]

For any of these conferences to be efficient and effective, the parties must have evaluated the relevant law and facts both before discovery, and once the discovery process has been exhausted, any pending motions or pleadings, and each party's strengths and weaknesses. Only after considering the evidence as a whole and where the arbitration hearing may lead may an attorney develop a strategy for what information or evidence should be excluded or included, what witnesses should be allowed or prohibited from testifying, or what visual aids would benefit or harm the proceeding.

These preliminary hearings allow the arbitrators to map out what the rest of the proceeding will or may look like so the parties can traverse it effectively, thoughtfully, and efficiently. If the parties can work out some of the "kinks" or "uncertainties" before the proceeding, the arbitration should be conducted more smoothly.

So a lot can be resolved during this preliminary conference to work out any potential bumps in the road. However, many times, even with the best intentions and planning, other disagreements pop up. Therefore, additional conferences may be required as discovery progresses and the arbitrator(s) must resolve discovery disputes, requests to amend claims or defenses, and determine the admissibility of evidence to be presented during the hearing. And even if an addition conference is not required, the issues may still need to be submitted to the arbi-

---

33. *Id.* at 18 (discussing Rule 16).
34. *Id.*

trators to resolve them. If a solo arbitrator presides, then that solo arbitrator will resolve any disagreement along the way and generally the parties agree to accept the arbitrator's ruling as final. If a panel of three arbitrators presides, then they can decide the issue collectively, by a majority, or more commonly, by one panelist who is appointed as Chair of the panel to resolve such disputes. How is the Chair appointed? Sometimes the three panelists decide and other times, the rules governing the arbitration will dictate how the Chair is chosen.

These disagreements can occur before or even during the hearing. Obviously, the goal is to resolve as many disputes as possible before the hearing in the preliminary conferences or even in conferences just before the hearing is to start. However, evidentiary issues and questions will arise during the hearing, and so the solo arbitrator or Chair will resolve those on the spot so that the hearing can move forward. It is also within the arbitrator or Chair's discretion to revisit a request during the proceeding, if necessary. And the decision of the arbitrators is final.

And it's not just discovery or evidentiary disagreements that may arise, more simple housekeeping issues, such as time limitations during the hearing, or scheduled lunches and breaks, may need to be ironed out as the hearing progresses.

The driving force behind these conferences or the arbitrators' on-the-spot decisions is fairness and efficiency of the proceedings.

Stop Points

1. Arbitration discovery is intended to be simpler and less burdensome than litigation. Some administering agency rules and court rules limit the depth and scope of discovery to keep it more proportionate to the claims in dispute.
2. The Federal Rules of Civil Procedure generally do not govern arbitrations specifically because it anticipates broader discovery designed for litigation. However, the purpose behind discovery—to level the playing field and ensure that each party has the documents and evidence to which it is entitled to support its claim or defense—does apply. Also, the rules requiring the parties act fairly and in good faith apply.
3. The Federal Rules of Evidence generally do not apply to arbitrations, except for claims of privilege and work product.
4. To increase the benefit of timeliness that arbitrations provide, some administering agency rules and parties have agreed to streamlined or expedited discovery to be completed within a shortened period of time.

5. Arbitrators will generally hold preliminary conferences with parties to work out the details of discovery depth, scope, and deadlines. These conferences may also address deadlines for motions, exchanging witness lists, etc.

6. When additional discovery or evidentiary issues arise after the preliminary conference, additional conferences may be held, the disputes submitted to the arbitrators for resolution, or the arbitrators may make a decision on the spot.

8. In-Person Hearing v. Telephonic/Virtual Appearance

In yet another effort to reduce costs and formalities, some arbitrations will not require an in-person hearing and instead may be resolved through document exchange and a hearing where the parties appear by telephone or computer.[35] Those requiring a full in-person hearing may be encouraged to be completed in just one to three days.[36] Although some may take longer, the idea is that arbitration should be quicker. And remember, because the arbitrators are usually paid for their time per day, the longer it takes to conduct the hearing, the higher the costs.

Therefore, if the parties' contract, administering agency rules, or the law does not dictate whether the hearing must be in-person or telephonic, the parties have yet another decision to make about which option would be best suited for their clients.

9. The Final Award: Content, Timing, Fees, and Compliance

Although we've already discussed the impact that a binding versus nonbinding arbitration has on the parties, there are still a few matters to address regarding the arbitrators' award: content, timing, fees, and compliance.

a. Content

The general rule is that unless the parties agree otherwise, the arbitrators will include brief reasons and explanations for their award. Because there are very limited grounds to appeal an arbitration decision,[37] there is less of a need to include detailed reasons. Also, some administering agencies require that the

---

35. AAA, *supra* note 8, at 2 (discussing the Streamlined Schedule).

36. *Id.*; JAMS COMPREHENSIVE ARBITRATION, *supra* note 4, at 3 (discussing Case Management Fees).

37. In addition to the reasons the Federal Arbitration Act gives for appealing an arbitration decision, some of the administering agencies will allow the parties to agree to an optional appeal process. JAMS COMPREHENSIVE ARBITRATION, *supra* note 4, at 32 (discussing Rule 34).

awards state whether the arbitrators consider it "final" for any necessary judicial proceedings.[38]

b. Timing

Additionally, most court rules and administering agency rules require an expeditious award once the hearing, either telephonic or in-person, is complete. This time period is usually within 14 days[39] to 30 days[40] after the hearing. Then there is a process for submitting the award to the parties to review for any errors, corrections, or clarifications. The parties are usually given a period of time in which to request such corrections, the arbitrators a period of time in which to respond or make such corrections, and then the award becomes final.[41]

c. Fees

Arbitration proceedings are not free. The parties must bear the cost of the arbitrators, hearing space, and administering agency, if hired. Unless agreed to otherwise by the parties, the fees will be shared equally among them.[42] However, as part of the arbitrators' award, those fees may be shifted to a party the arbitrators deem more responsible based on the outcome of the proceeding.[43]

d. Compliance

Once final, a binding arbitration award must be complied with by the parties. It amounts to a contract between them. Therefore, if a party does not fulfill its duties under the contract, the non-breaching party can take such steps as necessary to enforce the contract according to the Federal Arbitration Act or applicable state law.[44]

10. Confidentiality, Precedent, and Controlling Law

There are a few other important aspects of arbitration that need to be mentioned, even if only briefly: confidentiality, precedent, and the law that controls the arbitration.

---

38. CPR Rules, *supra* note 11, at 21–22 (discussing Rule 15.1).
39. AAA, *supra* note 8, at 11 (discussing Rule 30).
40. JAMS Comprehensive Arbitration, *supra* note 4, at 10 (discussing Rule 6(d)).
41. CPR Rules, *supra* note 11, at 22–23 (discussing Rule 15.6-7).
42. *Id.* at 24–25 (discussing Rules 18.2, 19.2).
43. *Id.*; JAMS Comprehensive Arbitration, *supra* note 4, at 27 (discussing Rule 24(f)).
44. JAMS Comprehensive Arbitration, *supra* note 4, at 28 (discussing Rule 25).

a. Confidentiality

Arbitration proceedings are confidential. So this can be both a pro and con for parties. Those who hope to keep a matter out of the public eye would see confidentiality as a plus, unlike litigation, where the claim becomes public the moment the plaintiff files the complaint. However, for those parties wanting to make a public statement about an issue, the confidentiality of the proceedings would be a negative. Regardless, the nature of arbitration proceedings is that they are to be confidential. In fact, rarely is a court reporter hired to transcribe an arbitration hearing unless the parties have agreed to an appeal process and therefore, have the need to create a record of the proceeding. However, unless this transcribed record is submitted to a court as part of the appeal, it would remain confidential.

b. Precedent

Regardless of whether the arbitration is binding or non-binding, the arbitrators' decision has no precedential value. Our legal system is built on "stare decisis" and precedent, which means that judges shouldn't reinvent the wheel; they should look at how other judges have already decided the same issue and rule consistently. That's why you spend so much time in law school learning how to research the law and apply that law to facts. You're training to think like lawyers and judges who do the exact same thing. A successful attorney would never go to court without researching the law impacting her client's case, and just hope that the judge will rule on the facts instead. And a successful judge would never just rule on the facts without evaluating how precedent would impact those facts to either dictate a certain result or suggest one.

The lack of precedent created by arbitration decisions means that a decision in one arbitration is not binding on a later one. The arbitrators treat each hearing on a case-by-case basis. For those parties wanting a quick resolution to their current dispute, the lack of precedential value of an arbitration decision may not matter. However, for those parties trying to create a pattern of results for certain legal disputes, that lack of precedential value may discourage them from participating in arbitration.

c. Controlling Law

The parties to an arbitration may agree to which jurisdiction's law governs the arbitration proceeding, and if not, the arbitrators are allowed to use the law as a guide, but to decide cases using the tenets of equity and common sense. So again, if a party wants to use case law to force a particular result, unless the parties have agreed to that law's controlling status, the arbitrators are not required to follow it.

In fact, arbitrators are also not bound by legal precedent when reaching their decisions and awards, but are only guided by it. That means that equity and fairness, and not the law, allow arbitrators to tailor remedies appropriate to each dispute. The benefit is that the arbitrators can identify creative and unique solutions to problems. The detriment is that arbitrators typically are not as generous with awards as juries would be. Why is that? A lot has to do with arbitrators being lawyers familiar with the legal process, so emotion and heart-felt appeals don't influence them as much. In fact, even though most arbitrators are permitted to award punitive damages, many do not because it takes a lot to shock their conscience or rise to the level of egregiousness. So the possibility of a smaller award is another trade-off for participating in arbitration to resolve your dispute more quickly than trial.

B. Mechanics Of Arbitration — The Wrap-Up

So that covers the majority of the ins and outs of the mechanics of arbitration, with the understanding that the rules are changing and being updated all of the time so that you should always check the rules of your jurisdiction or administering agency for the most current version. But hopefully you have a much better idea of what an arbitration may and can look like. It can be a very useful process to allow parties to resolve their disputes more quickly, easily, and cheaply than trial. It can be mandatory or voluntary, it can allow confidentiality and finality, and it can provide an advisory opinion if that is all the parties seek. And it can allow parties to "have their day in court" by engaging in a full in-person hearing. The parties can handle all of the details themselves, or hire an administering agency to do all of the "administrative" tasks, as well as be available to interpret rules and resolve issues on the spot. The parties may draft their own rules, borrow them from an administering agency, or create a hybrid. Unless dictated by contract, rule, or law, the parties can tailor an arbitration process best suited for their clients involved in this particular dispute. Therefore, arbitration has become a well-known, accepted, and respected alternative dispute resolution avenue that many parties must or have chosen to take.

Checkpoints

- Depending on the parties' contract, administering agency rules, or court rules, the arbitration hearing may be based on documents only with a supplemental hearing where the parties can appear by phone or virtually by computer. Otherwise, the hearing may be in person. However, if in person, the parties are usually encouraged to complete it within one to three days.

- The arbitrators' final award must be handed down in a timely manner once the hearing is completed. Usually, this must be within 7 to 30 days. The parties are then given a chance to point out any errors or corrections to be made to the award.

- Unless the parties agree otherwise, the award usually contains a brief explanation of the reasons behind the award.

- The arbitrators should designate whether the award is a "final" award for purposes of any related legal proceedings.

- The final award is a contract between the parties that must be followed or the non-breaching party may take action to have the contract enforced.

- Although the parties to an arbitration generally split the fees for the administering agency's service, arbitrators' rates, and room rental, arbitrators may apportion such fees differently as part of their award.

- Arbitrations are confidential proceedings and are therefore not open to the public.

- An award in one arbitration does not act as precedent in a later hearing. Each arbitration is decided on its own merits.

- There is no universal controlling law for arbitrations, and therefore the parties may agree to the law that will control, and if not, then the arbitrators may do so. However, arbitrators are generally not bound by legal precedent and can enter more creative awards to resolve the dispute than the law may allow. Additionally, arbitrators' awards may be less than a jury verdict because arbitrators are less swayed by emotion and heart-felt pleas.

Chapter 5

An Arbitration Hearing Under the Microscope

Roadmap

- Some arbitration hearings are based on documents and a telephonic hearing, while others are in-person. For the in-person hearings, there are many aspects that are similar to a traditional trial, such as opening statements, direct and cross-examinations, objections, evidence, and summations or closing arguments.

- One difference between an arbitration hearing and a trial is that the arbitrators may ask the attorneys questions during their opening statements and summations.

Now that we've reviewed all of the nuts and bolts of what makes an arbitration what it is, it's time to move on to what an arbitration hearing actually looks like and how it proceeds. So let's revisit one of the scenarios from earlier in this book. In the example from the mediation chapter, Sam Hanson caused a car accident that injured Mary Thompson. After receiving treatment for her injuries for 6 to 9 months, Mary's doctors determined that she would be left with some permanent damage and limitations in her back, but that the rest of her injuries have healed. Assuming negotiation and mediation have proven unsuccessful with Sam's insurance company, Mary and her attorney need to decide what to do next: file a lawsuit or request arbitration. If suit is filed, crowded court dockets could make it a year or more before Mary gets a trial date. And for Mary, she's already waited almost a year just to file the lawsuit—now she may have to wait another year to get her day in court?

So why arbitration? As Mary's attorney, you explained to her that although there are rules and timeframes that arbitrators must work within, you won't have to contend with packed court dockets and so the discovery process can be completed and the hearing date scheduled much more quickly. And since Mary has already had to wait almost a year to "recover" from her injuries, she may not want to wait any longer.

Now, you may also explain to Mary that although she was firm in her conviction to file a lawsuit when she first met with you just a few days after the accident, her conviction seems to have diminished over time after all of the doctors' visits, treatment, and pain she's suffered. And even if Mary's conviction has increased over time too, arbitration gives her a different option if she chooses.

Now, Mary's conviction may have been based on wanting to have her "day in court" while at the same time stopping the meter on her legal fees and costs. You explain that because an arbitration hearing is a less formal "trial," Mary can testify, present witnesses, submit evidence, and put on her case to the arbitrators. If Mary is motivated to tell her side of the story to the "judge," then an arbitration can provide that similar experience.

Also, because an arbitration hearing can usually be scheduled much sooner than getting a trial date, it will cost Mary less in attorney's fees (the amount attorneys make per hour for their legal service) and costs (any money the attorney pays on the client's behalf to pursue or defend the client's claim like postage, copies, messenger services, expert witness fees, travel expenses, etc.) For clients paying their attorney's fee by the hour, this could be a huge savings, even though it may not be for those clients paying their attorneys through a contingency fee contract (where the attorney is paid a percentage of the client's recovery from a settlement, jury trial, or arbitration decision). However, for clients with an hourly or contingency fee arrangement, the costs involved in an arbitration are lower than trial. How so? If the parties can schedule the arbitration hearing at a mutually agreeable time when each side's witnesses are more readily available to testify, then travel costs may be lower. Also, because the case will not be presented to a jury, you don't need to be elaborate or flashy, because it will not impress the arbitrators. For arbitration hearings, the exhibits and evidence needed to prove or defend the case need to be simple and straightforward. In fact, even enlargements of documents may not be necessary for the arbitrators who may have copies of the actual documents in front of them during the hearing.

Lastly, you explain to Mary that arbitration proceedings are typically private and confidential. If Mary is trying to make a public statement on an issue, then an arbitration proceeding will not be the best choice. But if the parties are looking to resolve a heated dispute outside the public's watchful eye, then arbitration may be just the right option.

And many times, if parties choose to arbitrate, it's because they have already tried negotiation and/or mediation and it has not been successful. And you remind Mary that the negotiation and mediation were not successful in her case and so now it's decision time: arbitration or litigation. And although litigation may still be an option if Mary chooses non-binding arbitration, she, Sam, and Sam's insurance company may decide to accept the non-binding award and have the case resolved sooner.

Mary agrees to arbitrate, and so assuming the commencement documents were properly filed, arbitrators chosen, rules agreed upon, discovery completed, etc., the parties are ready to start the in-person hearing, and so let's take a close examination of what that looks like.

I. The Arbitration Hearing—Procedure

Unlike negotiations and mediations that do not follow a strict structure or flow, because they progress based on the parties, mediators, emotions, offers, and demands, arbitrations do follow a common structure. Because arbitrations are similar in nature to a trial, many of the same aspects or segments that comprise a trial are also present during an arbitration: preliminary matters, opening statements, direct examination of witnesses, cross-examination of witnesses, exhibit presentations, closing statements, and motions. Because of this accepted structure and organization, we can delve a little deeper into the details of each segment to help you better understand what happens, when, and why during an arbitration hearing.

II. Preliminary Matters

Although most preliminary matters are addressed as described above in preliminary or scheduling conferences, some matters are taken up just before the hearing begins. These might be minor housekeeping or timing matters that did not arise until then, such as a witness' unforeseen travel delays, or a change in circumstances of one of the parties. So just like a judge, the arbitrator(s) may resolve a few matters just before the hearing begins, with the intent to have the hearing run smoothly and fairly for all involved.

The arbitrators' rulings are to be followed both before and during the hearing. However, it's also possible that the arbitrators may make temporary rulings to be revisited during the hearing. But the attorneys are to follow those rulings until and unless the rulings change during a revisit.

III. Opening Statements

Because arbitrations are initiated by one party usually referred to as the claimant or plaintiff, the claimant presents its opening statement first, followed by the party or parties being brought to arbitration called the respondent or defendant. Just like at a trial, the opening statement is designed to tell the story of what occurred between or among the involved parties to cause the dispute and what the party is seeking to remedy that "wrong." Also like a trial, the opening statement should avoid argument and instead should convey what will be presented through witnesses, testimony, and exhibits expected to be introduced during the hearing. Depending on the local rules and preferences of the arbitration panel, opening statements may be limited in time, scope, and content.

A. What to Exclude from an Opening Statement

As discussed above, the arbitrators' decisions and rulings from the prehearing and scheduling conferences control during the hearing itself. If a decision was made during the preliminary matters to exclude certain witnesses, testimony, or exhibits, the parties must refrain from mentioning such matters during their opening statements, and the opposing party should object (a formal way of interrupting the other side and letting the arbitration panel know that mention was made of an excluded matter) to allow the arbitration panel to decide how to proceed.

In jury trials, attorneys must avoid mentioning evidence the judge excluded from trial and must object immediately if the opposing attorney does mention excluded evidence.[1] Mentioning excluded evidence is the type of mistake that can cause a mistrial. Why? Because it is crucial that jurors not learn of excluded evidence because it is evidence the judge has determined not credible, too prejudicial, or not supported. And even if a judge tells the jurors to disregard or forget about what they just heard, there remains the possibility the jurors will place more emphasis on it or not be able to forget it. However, when attorneys comprise an arbitration panel, the fear of unfair or undue emphasis being placed on an excluded matter is avoided because the panel is similarly trained to only consider relevant and non-excluded evidence in its decisions. This example highlights how the rules of evidence are loosened or less strictly applied in arbitration hearings because the potential harm for an unfair decision is not present.

However, even though the fear of contaminating the jury is not present during an arbitration hearing when excluded evidence is mentioned, it still vio-

---

1. Fed. R. Evid. 403.

lates the arbitration panel's ruling. Arbitrators are human beings and much of their decision-making is discretionary. Therefore, an attorney who ignores an arbitration panel's rulings may lose credibility with the panel and have the panel's discretionary decisions favor the opponents. Again, just because an arbitration hearing is slightly different than a trial, the rules of professional conduct and ethics control all lawyers in both proceedings.[2]

B. What to Include in an Opening Statement

Just as important as what to exclude from an opening statement is what to include: a theme or theory that encapsulates your client's case, which means the essence of the dispute from your client's perspective through which all of the evidence can be viewed, held together, and better understood. For instance, if your client is an individual and the opponent is an insurance company, your theme might be some version of David versus Goliath, or profits over people. However, whatever theme or theory you decide upon must actually suit the facts and evidence in your case. Clever mottos and slogans do not win arbitration hearings or trials; solid evidence and law do. However, holding a case together, particularly complicated or complex ones, with a simple and easily understandable and defensible theme can make it much easier for the arbitration panel, and judges and juries, to follow and agree with.

The only way to craft an effective theme is to know your case inside and out and anticipate the other side's strategy and plans to poke holes in your claims or defenses. Sometimes themes can come to an attorney early in the representation process, and others develop over time as more evidence and information is discovered and processed. And for a theme to be effective, it must run through the entire hearing from opening statement, through direct and cross-examinations, exhibit presentations, and closing statements. If only part of the case is supported by the theme, then it is not a solid theme. Just because an arbitration hearing has some differences to a negotiation, mediation, and trial, the basics of strong and effective communication are still present — tell the audience what you are going to tell them, tell them, and then tell them what you told them. A degree of repetition is necessary for the audience to fol-

---

2. "Litigation is not just advocacy. Legal and ethical rules define how pretrial litigation is practiced and constrain your conduct.... A knowledge of the law and ethics of [arbitration will tell you what you are required, forbidden, or permitted to do} but it will not tell you whether pursuing a particular course is a good idea." J. Alexander Tanford & Layne S. Keele, THE PRETRIAL PROCESS 1 (2d ed. 2012).

low and remember the information being provided. An effective theme is woven through each portion of the hearing, sometimes subtly and sometimes more overtly to remind the audience that your client's position is the prevailing one factually, legally, and even morally.

You read that right: "morally." So although you have heard that lawyers must be professional and ethical, how does being moral fit in? Well, arbitrators are human beings, not robots, so if an attorney can show the panel that the client's position is both logically correct (through law and facts) to appeal to the arbitrator's mind, and morally correct (it is the right thing to do because of fairness, equity, etc.) to appeal to the arbitrator's heart, the theme is a strong one. Generally, people want to do what they know is right and feel is right.

C. Prepare to Answer Questions During Opening Statements

During opening statements at trial, the judge and jury sit passively, listen, and observe. However, during the opening statements of an arbitration hearing, the arbitrators may ask counsel questions about the law and facts. And just like with any exchange between attorneys and the decision-makers, the more conversational the exchange is, the more effective it will be. No one enjoys being lectured to, and from attending classes or seminars, you have probably realized that those professors and speakers who make it seem like you are in their living room having an engaging intellectual conversation with them are those who you most pay attention to and retain the information they provide. Those who just lecture or demand you understand the information they are discussing are less likely to stimulate your intellect or cause you to remember what they said.

The size of the hearing room can aid to the conversational feel if all involved are seated at a large conference table or closer quarters than an expansive courtroom. The idea is not to yell or lecture to the arbitrators, but to answer their questions like you're happy they asked. If the arbitrators are asking questions, it means they are listening and engaged and have thought through some of the issues and would like clarification now to help them process the rest of the proceeding. Although many attorneys would prefer not to be interrupted during their presentation, being asked questions is a good thing because it allows attorneys to address what's on the arbitrators' minds and not just what the attorneys thought the arbitrators were concerned about.

An effective theme will also assist in answering these questions persuasively because you will have a foundation or touchstone on which to ground your responses. If your theme is a strong one, then no matter what question is asked, you will be able to view it through your theme and your answer will support the theme. So for instance, if your theme is profits over people, and you represent the "people," then regardless of the question you are asked, first think about how the question relates to profits being put above people and how your response will further support that idea through the law and facts that will be presented during the hearing. And the same is true for the respondent who wants to rebut the claimant's theme by answering the arbitrators' questions to show how the case does not support putting profits over people but instead supports the respondent's theme.

D. Order of the Opening Statements

Claimants or plaintiffs who file the claim or arbitration notice will present their opening statement first. Then, depending on the local rules, arbitrators' preference, or parties' preference, the respondent or defendant may present its opening statement immediately following the claimant's or wait until the claimant presents its case (generally called a case-in-chief), but before the respondent presents its side (or its case-in-chief/rebuttal of claimant's case).

By waiting until after the claimant's case-in-chief to conduct opening statement, the respondent can keep its theme fresh in the arbitrators' minds before putting on its first witness. It can present a different way of looking at what has been presented thus far and give the arbitrators a different theme on which to rely.

However, by not presenting its opening statement immediately after the claimant's, the respondent loses the chance to share its theme and theory of the case with the arbitrators' mind from the hearing's outset. Generally, respondents will present their opening statement directly after the claimant's because they don't want to wait that long for the panel to hear their theme and theory of the case. Remember that a strong theme sets the stage for the rest of the proceeding through each stage—direct examinations, cross-examinations, exhibit presentations, objections, and closing arguments. By sharing that theme early on, attorneys can strengthen and support it through each question asked of witnesses, each objection made and responded to, and each piece of evidence introduced.

There are benefits to both approaches, so if the local rules, arbitrators, or parties allow a respondent to decide when to present its opening statement, it could be a strategic decision to the case. However, regardless of the order of the opening statements, the rules of what to exclude, what to include, and being prepared to answer questions apply to all opening statements.

IV. Direct Examination

The next step in the hearing is the presentation of witnesses through direct examination. Claimants present their witnesses first, the respondent may cross-examine, and the claimant may conduct redirect examination.[3] After the claimant presents all its witnesses and exhibits, the respondent or respondents then present their witnesses by conducting direct examination, the claimant may cross-examine, and the respondent can conduct redirect examination. So both sides follow the same general format when presenting their witnesses.

So what is direct examination? Direct examination is the attorney's chance to ask questions to a witness to elicit that witness's knowledge of facts about the claim. A strong direct examination is one where those observing feel like they are listening to an engaging conversation between two people revealing lots of relevant information about the case. Usually normal conversations don't follow strict guidelines or structure: people interrupt each other, finish each other's sentences, veer off on tangents, or get distracted by other events. However, an effective direct examination should follow more of a structure so that the arbitrators can follow along with what is happening and why, rather than feeling like they're watching a tennis match with balls being hit back and forth, out of bounds, or hitting the net. The attorney asking the questions is in fact "directing" the witness to topics and issues that the attorney wants the witness to address. The attorney and witnesses have usually practiced or discussed the topics and questions before the day of the hearing to prepare for a smoother and understandable "conversation" in front of the arbitrators.

So, for instance, a direct examination of our car accident victim Mary might go something like this:

Mary's Attorney (MA): Good afternoon, Ms. Thompson. Would you please introduce yourself to the panel and explain briefly why you're here today?

Mary (M): Yes, good afternoon. I'm Mary Thompson and I'm here because I was involved in a car accident last year with Sam Hanson. I was injured in the accident and have been trying to get Mr. Hanson's insurance company to pay me for those injuries.

---

3. In some hearings, arbitrators may also permit re-cross-examination and additional redirect examination, but we will limit the discussion to the direct, cross, and redirect for simplicity.

MA: Okay, Mary, before we get into the details of the accident and your injuries, could you tell the panel a little bit about yourself in terms of where you live and where you work?

M: Sure. I was born and raised here in Greenville and have never left. And I work at Greenville Energy.

MA: Let's start with living in Greenville. You said you lived here all your life. Do you have family here?

M: Yes, my parents and two brothers also live in town.

MA: Are you married?

M: Yes, I am, and I have two children.

MA: Tell us a little bit about your husband and children.

M: Bill Thompson is my husband and we got married 15 years ago and we have a wonderful son Mike, who is 12 years old, and a beautiful daughter Patty, who is 10 years old.

MA: Now you said you worked at Greenville Energy. What do you do there?

M: I'm the assistant project manager of residential energy. That means I'm responsible for a team of 16 employees to implement plans to improve providing residential energy in the community.

MA: How long have you worked there?

M: 18 years.

[There may be additional questions about Mary's general background information so that the panel gets a little feel for who she is and she gets to build a rapport with them.]

MA: Mary, I'd now like to turn your attention to the car accident that we're here about today. When did the accident happen?

M: It was July 4 of last year.

MA: What time?

MA: It was in the morning, around 10 o'clock.

MA: Where did the accident happen?

M: It was here in Greenville at the intersection of Main Street and 14th Avenue North.

MA: Is there a traffic light at that intersection?

M: Yes, there is.

MA: Just before the accident, what street were you driving on?

M: I was driving east on Main Street, approaching the intersection with 14th Ave. North.

MA: How many lanes of traffic does Main Street have?

M: Two lanes total, one in each direction.

MA: You said you were driving east on Main Street. Where were you coming from?

M: I had just visited my friend Liz in the hospital.

MA: What hospital was that?

M: Greenville Memorial Hospital on Madison Street.

MA: After you left the hospital, where were you going?

M: I went to Paula's Bakery to pick up a cake for Mike's birthday.

MA: And is that your son Mike?

M: Yes.

MA: What time did you go to Paula's Bakery?

M: I picked up the cake around 9:45 that morning.

MA: Where were you headed after the bakery?

M: I was headed home for my son Mike's birthday party.

MA: As you're heading east on Main Street approaching the intersection with 14th Avenue North, what color was the traffic light for you?

M: It had just turned green.

MA: When you drove into the intersection, what color was the traffic light for you?

M: It was green.

MA: Were there any cars in front of you as you drove into the intersection?

M: Yes, there was a large white van that was in front of me and drove into the intersection first.

MA: What happened as you drove into the intersection?

M: A car drove through the intersection on my left, slammed my car on the driver's door, and spun my car around.

MA: After your car spun, where did it end up?

M: I smashed into a telephone pole on the southeast corner of the intersection.

MA: Do you know what direction the car that hit you came from?

M: Yes, it was driving south on 14th Avenue.

[The direct examination would go on to discuss Mary's injuries, medical treatment, limitations at work and in daily activities.]

Note a couple of things about this direct examination: First, the attorney tries to let the client do a good amount of talking, because it's the client's story, not the attorney's. Second, notice the sign-posting (signaling a change in topic or issue) and dovetailing (using part of the witness's answer within a later question) the attorney uses in the questions.

As a sign-post example, Mary's attorney said, "I'd now like to turn your attention to the car accident that we're here about today." This is a clear shift from Mary's background information into another specific topic, the accident. As for a dovetail example, after Mary explained that she had been born and raised in town and worked at Greenville Energy, the attorney asked "Let's start with living in Greenville ... Do you have family here?" and then later used the other portion of the answer to ask, "Now you said you worked at Greenville Energy, what do you do there?"

These techniques highlight the direction and flow of the client's story, keep the arbitrators focused on the topics being discussed, and Mary's attorney engaged in the client's story. The direct examination becomes an interesting conversation between attorney and witness that goes to support that side's theory of the case.

Now, earlier, I discussed the importance of a theme to hold the case together and that a solid theme should weave through each stage of the arbitration hearing. Although that's absolutely true, that does not mean the theme can be subtly or overtly highlighted in every question and every answer. So assuming Mary's attorney was using the "profits over people" theme, the attorney may not be able to address that theme until later questions about the client's injuries, the extent of her physical limitations, her outstanding medical bills, lost wages, etc., to build the case that as a "person," Mary is more than just numbers and she's entitled to be put back the way she was before the accident that was caused by the other side. However, even though every question doesn't address the "profits over people" theme specifically, there are still some questions that must be asked to put the direct examination in context and transition between topics, such as Mary's background information.

And the direct examinations for all witnesses for both sides would proceed generally the same way, with the attorney conducting the direct focusing that witness's testimony to what he/she knows about the claim or defense. And to be clear, that may mean that witness X may only give testimony about the color of the traffic light at the time of the accident, witness Y may only give testimony about Mary's back pain, and witness Z may only give testimony about how much Mary's medical bills are because that is what each witness has knowledge about. Not every witness can testify as to every aspect of the claim or defense.

V. Cross-Examination

So after one side conducts a direct examination of its witness, the opposing side gets to conduct a cross-examination. What's the difference? Well, the purpose of cross-examination is to elicit testimony that will help the opponent's position, or undermine or highlight inconsistencies in the witness's testimony. Generally on cross-examination, the attorney asking the questions does more of the talking and tries to limit the witness's answers to yes or no. However, sometimes the attorney will encourage the witness to give further explanation because the witness's version of events may become less credible or believable because it changes, becomes too extreme, or contradicts previous statements.

When conducting a cross-examination, attorneys should again keep their theme or theory in mind to ensure that the information elicited from the witness supports the theme or theory, undermines the opponent's theme or theory, or discredits the witness as a credible source of information.

Using the example of Mary's direct examination above, here is what a few cross-examination questions from Sam Hanson's insurance company[4] might look like:

Insurance Attorney (IA): Good afternoon, Ms. Thompson. I represent ABC Insurance Company and am going to ask you some questions about the car accident that we're here about today.

M: Okay.

IA: You stated you were driving east on Main Street just before the accident, correct?

M: Yes.

---

4. Note if this were a jury trial, the jury would not be told that Sam had insurance and was not paying the claim out of his own pocket. The jury would be told that Sam was being sued as an individual. The reason is to allow juries to assess the plaintiff's claim accurately without thinking "Oh, we can give Mary a lot more money because an insurance company is paying her, not Sam." However, in arbitrations, the truth that Mary's claim is actually being paid by an insurance company may be revealed because the arbitrators will not be swayed by that reality.

IA: And you had made two stops before the accident?

M: Yes.

IA: One was to Greenville General Hospital to visit Liz, your friend?

M: Yes.

IA: And the other was to Paula's Bakery to pick up your son's birthday cake?

M: Yes, that's right.

IA: I want to talk about your friend Liz first. Is Liz a close friend?

M: She's my very closest friend.

IA: How long have you been friends?

M: We grew up together. Gosh, we've known each other since grade school, so over 25 years.

IA: The morning of the accident when you went to visit Liz in the hospital, how long were you there?

M: About an hour.

IA: How was Liz's mood that morning?

M: She was in a lot of pain, so she was pretty down.

IA: And you must have been pretty upset to see your closest friend in so much pain?

M: Of course. It broke my heart that she was hurting and that I couldn't do anything about it but cry along with her and be there for her.

IA: Now after you left the hospital from visiting Liz, you went to Paula's Bakery around 9:45?

M: Yes to pick up my son's birthday cake.

IA: And your son's birthday party was that same day, right?

M: Yes, it was starting at noon.

IA: And were there still things to do to get ready for the party?

M: Oh yes, lots of things to do.

IA: So it's safe to say that after you picked up Mike's cake, you needed to get home to get ready for the party.

M: Yes.

IA: You said that Mr. Hanson's car came from your left, correct?

M: Yes, he hit me on my driver's side door, which is on my left.

IA: But prior to the impact, you didn't see the car, did you?

M: No, not until Mr. Hanson hit me.

IA: So you don't know for sure which direction Mr. Hanson was driving?

M: I assume it was south on 14th because of how he hit me.

IA: But to be clear, you don't know that for sure?

M: No.

IA: You also stated that there was a white van that was driving in front of you and entered the intersection first, correct?

M: Yes.

IA: No one has been able to track down that van, have they?

M: No, but I saw it.

IA: So other than your statement about the white van driving in front of you, to your knowledge no one else saw that van, correct?

M: There was a van, I saw it.

IA: Ms. Thompson, again, other than your statement about the white van, to your knowledge no one else saw the van, correct?

M: Correct.

IA: And at the time of the accident, you had a lot on your mind, correct?

M: No, I didn't, I know what happened.

IA: But to be clear, just before the accident, you had visited with your best friend who was in a lot of physical and emotional pain and that upset you, and you needed to get home to prepare for your son's birthday party that was to start in just a short time?

M: Well, yes.

[Again, the cross-examination would go on with the attorney trying to determine whether Mary was at least partially responsible for the accident, whether her claimed injuries were a result of the accident or pre-existing, whether Mary did all she could have done to heal from her injuries, etc.]

Here, the attorney has tried to emphasize that Mary's mind may have been preoccupied with other matters, like her best friend's medical condition and rushing home to prepare for her son's birthday party, and that her recollection of the accident may be different from what actually happened. The attorney did this by using Mary's own testimony from her direct examination about what she had done before the accident. Also, the attorney committed Mary to her testimony that she didn't see Mr. Hanson's car until he hit her, and therefore highlighted that she may not know what direction he was driving from. And the accuracy of Mary's memory was further called into question because of the white van that no one else saw.

And again, the purpose of cross-examination is for the opponent to call the witness's credibility into question, to help bolster the opponent's theme and theory of the case, or to highlight inconsistencies in the claimant's case.

VI. Redirect Examination

So what does Mary's attorney have left to do after a cross-examination like that? That's where redirect examination comes into play, which is Mary's attorney's chance to rehabilitate her credibility and the accuracy of her story. The scope or content of redirect examination is limited to matters brought out on cross-examination. Therefore, Mary's attorney could not ask her questions about things that were never raised in cross-examination, but could try to fix some of the damage the opponent's attorney caused by questioning how well Mary remembers the details of the accident, and may go something like this:

Mary's Attorney (MA): Mary, I'd like to ask you a few follow-up questions about what you were just discussing with Attorney X. How long did it take you to get from the hospital to the bakery?

Mary (M): About 10 minutes, if that.

MA: What time did you leave the hospital that morning?

MA: Well, I left my friend Liz at 9, but I didn't leave the hospital until around 9:30 or so.

MA: What did you do for those 30 minutes?

M: I went down to the cafeteria to get something to eat and have some coffee. I wanted to clear my head and get myself together before going to pick up Mike's cake.

MA: Did you do anything else during those 30 minutes?

M: Yes, I went to the hospital chapel to say a prayer for Liz.

MA: How was your mood when you left the hospital?

M: I was in good spirits.

MA: After you picked up the cake, were you in a rush to get home?

M: No. The cake was my last errand that morning, so I was headed home after that, but not in a rush.

MA: Why weren't you in a rush?

M: There were about 10 people there setting up for the party, including my parents, my brothers and their families, and some friends.

MA: How many people were coming to the party?

M: Just our family, a few friends, and 5 of Mike's friends.

MA: Now, turning to the accident itself, how sure are you that there was a white van in front of you?

M: Very sure.

MA: What makes you say that?

M: Well, I had been driving east on Main Street for about 2 miles or so, and the van had been in front of me that whole time. So I noticed it again when I saw the light turn green for us and the van went through the intersection first.

MA: Thank you, Mary. No further questions.

So here, Mary's attorney has tried to show that Mary did have a clear head and was not in a rush at the time of the accident. The attorney may have also redirected Mary on other matters too, but this example was meant to highlight the areas where the opponent focused on undermining Mary's memory and recollection of the accident.

VII. Objections

Although objections were discussed briefly above as they relate to keeping out evidence that the arbitrators excluded during opening statements, objections are also relevant to be made during direct, cross, and redirect examinations. In addition to keeping out excluded testimony during examinations, objections can exclude evidence that does not comply with the rules of evidence. Just because the evidence or testimony is being presented to arbitrators and not a jury, the evidence should be credible, authentic, relevant, and not too prejudicial to the proceedings. Therefore, the rules of evidence apply to at least guide the arbitrators and attorneys as to what evidence is admissible.

However, the rules may be less strictly applied because many of the dangers in presenting evidence to jurors are not present.

So, for example, hearsay evidence is generally excluded from trial unless is fits into one of the recognized exceptions, like an admission by the opposing party or an excited utterance. Hearsay evidence is defined as "an out of court statement being offered for the truth of the matter asserted."[5] What does that mean? It means that one side is trying to admit an oral or written statement made prior to the hearing or trial, during the hearing or trial, for the purpose of the statement being taken or accepted as true. The concern with these types of statements is that if there is not a recognized exception, the statements may not be credible or authenticated.

So let's say that Sam's insurance company wants to have one of Mary's fellow employees testify that he overheard Mary's husband say, "Since the accident, Mary isn't as hurt as she says. She can pretty much do everything she could before the accident." First, because the employee heard the statement at some time before the hearing, it's an out of court statement. Second, the insurance company wants to introduce the statement to prove that it's true, that Mary isn't as hurt as she says she is. So it meets the definition of hearsay. However, it doesn't fit into one of the exceptions because even though Mary allegedly said it and she's the opposing party to the insurance company, it was Mary's husband who made the statement and he's not an opposing party. So although the statement would clearly be excluded from the jury because it's hearsay that doesn't fall into an exception, it may be allowed at an arbitration hearing, because the arbitrators should not be swayed by the statement lacking credibility or authenticity.

In fact, some arbitrators may even directly or strongly suggest to the attorneys to refrain from making objections throughout the hearing so it may run more smoothly. Why would arbitrators do this? Because unlike a trial, where a court reporter transcribes the proceedings and the attorneys create a record to use on appeal, the arbitration hearing is not being transcribed and it's not, unless for the limited circumstances discussed in the previous chapter section 10(a), being prepared for appeal. Further, most arbitrators are lawyers. They understand the purpose behind the rules of evidence to avoid prejudicing a jury or allowing unreliable testimony to contaminate the jury's verdict. The arbitrators can assess the appropriate weight and credibility to the testimony so that their decision is fair and supported.

And other times, making objections is discretionary. For instance, the insurance company's last cross-examination question to Mary is a compound question, meaning it includes more than one question. The attorney asked

---

5. Fed. R. Evid. 801(a)–(c).

"But to be clear, just before the accident, you had visited with your best friend who was in a lot of physical and emotional pain and that upset you, and you needed to get home to prepare for your son's birthday party that was to start in just a short time?" That question asked about visiting Mary's friend, the friend's pain, Mary being upset, and Mary being in a rush to get home for her son's party. Mary's attorney could have objected to that being a compound question, which would require that the question be broken up. However, would that have helped Mary's case to have do so? Here's how it might look:

> Insurance Attorney (IA): But to be clear, just before the accident, you had visited with your best friend who was in a lot of physical and emotional pain and that upset you, and you needed to get home to prepare for your son's birthday party that was to start in just a short time?
>
> Mary's Attorney (MA): Objection, compound question.
>
> Arbitrators: Sustained. Please rephrase.
>
> IA: Yes, thank you. Ms. Thompson, just before the accident, you had visited your friend in the hospital?
>
> M: Yes.
>
> IA: And your friend was in a lot of pain?
>
> M: Yes.
>
> IA: Physical pain?
>
> M: Yes.
>
> IA: Emotional pain?
>
> M: Yes.
>
> IA: And that made you upset for your friend?
>
> M: Yes, of course.
>
> IA: Then you went to the bakery?
>
> M: Yes.
>
> IA: To pick up your son's cake?
>
> M: Yes.
>
> IA: For his party that started at noon that day?
>
> M: Yes.
>
> IA: It was about 9:45 when you picked up the cake?
>
> M: Yes.

So although Mary's attorney was absolutely correct that it was a compound question, when it gets broken down into all of these shorter, individual questions, it can actually sound a lot worse like Mary had way too many things on her mind to have been fully accurate in her recollection of the accident. So choosing when and whether to object is also a strategy in arbitration and trial.

VIII. Exhibits And Evidence

Throughout the direct, cross, and redirect examinations, the attorneys may also introduce physical evidence like copies of Mary's medical records and bills, enlarged photographs of the intersection and damage to both Mary and Sam's cars, x-ray and MRI films, correspondence between the parties, etc. As stated before, not every witness can testify about every aspect of the claim or defense, not every witness is knowledgeable with the evidence to be able to testify about it. So lawyers will have certain witnesses testify and verify certain documents. So Mary would be able to testify about the photographs of the intersection and damage to her car, and some of her medical records and bills. However, Mary's doctors would be better suited to introduce the X-ray and MRI results and explain what they mean, discuss more details of certain medical records, and Mary's likelihood of a complete recovery.

Because arbitration hearings are less formal than trials, arbitrators may handle the admission of exhibits and documents differently. Similar to preparing for trial, the attorneys may exchange exhibits before the hearing to see if they can agree on some or all being admitted during the hearing. If so, then that makes for a smoother hearing because the attorneys will not be trying to keep the evidence out.

Other arbitrators may want to the attorneys to exchange exhibits so that each side is aware of what the other plans to admit and prepare for any objections to raise during the hearing when the evidence is introduced.

And just as objections may be appropriate for witness's testimony during the hearing, they may be just as appropriate for exhibits or documents being admitted. Remember that hearsay applies to both oral and written statements made out of court. Therefore, all documents, photographs, records, etc. drafted or created before the arbitration hearing fall into this category. And just like oral statements, if these written statements are admitted to show the information they contain is true, then they are hearsay and are inadmissible unless they fall within an exception. So, like the oral statement example above, the arbitrators may resolve evidence disputes in one of several different ways: 1) require the attorneys to work out any concerns before the hearing during the document and exhibit exchange; 2) have the arbitrators rule on any objections to evidence before rather than during the hearing; 3) require the attorneys to raise any unresolved objections during the hearing at the time the evidence is introduced; or 4) even direct or discourage objections from being made during the hearing with the understanding that any harm the evidence could have caused a jury is not present in an arbitration.

The point is that claims and defenses require proof and support. That proof comes in the form of testimony, evidence, and documents; however, for that proof to support a claim or defense, it must be reliable and credible. Arbitrators' rulings, the attorneys' motions to exclude or admit evidence, and objections all work to ensure that only such reliable and credible proof is considered when reaching a decision.

IX. Closing Statements/Summations

Like a bookend to the arbitration hearing, opening statements start the proceedings and closing statements or summations end them. The biggest difference between the two are that summations contain more certainty about the evidence because it has actually been presented, and are more argumentative about whether the legal standards in the claim or defenses were met.

A. Theme or Theory

Like the opening, the summation should use the same theme or theory chosen, because if it's a solid theme, it holds the whole case together from beginning to end. However, unlike the opening where the attorney lays out the story that he/she plans to present through witnesses and evidence, the summation is a walk-through and confirmation of what that testimony and evidence was and how it proved exactly what the attorney said it would from the outset. The summation will also highlight the inconsistencies and weaknesses of the opponent's case to further support the attorney's own case, because the cross-examinations have been completed and the attorney can remind the panel all of the things the witnesses said that hurt that witness's credibility or the opponent's position in the case.

However, again like the opening statement, a good structure and flow to the summation is crucial. The sage advice of "Tell them what you plan to tell them, tell them, and then tell them what you told them" is applicable here. Using your theme, structure and organize the summation so that it hits all of the main points necessary to prove your side of the case. So Mary's attorney's summation using the Profits over People theme, may look something like this:

"Good afternoon, panel. This may seem like a simple case of a car accident where a woman was injured, but it's more than that, it's a case of profits being put above people. You've met Mary Thompson, who was driving through an intersection on a green light when her car was T-boned by Sam Hanson, who was speeding and ran a red light. Despite all of Mary's debilitating and well-documented injuries, ABC Insurance Company wants to keep its money in its pocket rather than compensating Mary for what happened. And today's arbitration proved that Mr. Hanson was responsible for causing the accident, that Mary suffered significant injuries because of the accident, and that ABC Insurance Company is required to, but has not, properly compensated her because its bottom line is more important than putting Mary back to where she was before the accident.

"First, let's review the evidence proving that Sam Hanson was solely responsible for this accident. He admitted to...."

Based on the lawyer's introduction to his summation, the rest of the closing would cover those three topics—Mr. Hanson's liability, Mary's injuries and the cost to compensate her for those injuries, and the insurance company's failure to pay, which increases its profits the longer it keeps any money that should be paid out in claims.

Now, at trial, the general order of closing arguments is plaintiff, defendant, and then plaintiff's rebuttal argument. What is a rebuttal argument? It's the plaintiff's last say in the case by allowing the plaintiff to directly rebut issues or matters raised by the defendant during the defendant's closing argument. Usually the time for a rebuttal argument is shorter than the main closing argument and it's limited to matters raised in the defendant's closing argument, which mirrors the purpose and scope of redirect examinations explained above.

However, depending on the jurisdiction, arbitrators' preferences, or even the attorneys' preferences, it's possible for the respondent/defendant to present its summation first and then the claimant/plaintiff, in which case the claimant's entire closing is a rebuttal as well as an affirmative summation. Strategically, there are pros and cons to choosing either order for the summations, but as stated many times in this book, the answer to which order should or must be followed is "it depends."

B. Prepare to Answer Questions During Summation

Just like the opening statements, the arbitrators may ask the attorneys questions during their summations, so be prepared. Attorneys should view questions as a way to directly address an arbitrator's concern. Remember, the arbitrators are deciding how to resolve the dispute, so if they need more information to do so, attorneys should be willing to provide it when asked.

Because the summations represent the culmination of the entire arbitration proceeding, this is the attorneys' final chance to cement their case or defense and clear up any ambiguities or confusion. If an arbitrator takes the time to ask a question, the attorney should take the time to answer it completely, honestly, and an a way that is consistent with the attorney's theme.

X. Conclusion

Arbitration is usually the last of the alternative dispute resolution processes in which attorneys will engage, but it can be a faster and easier way to resolve a claim than trial. But before participating in an arbitration, attorneys need to consider a list of concerns described in Part I: whether the client signed a contract with a mandatory arbitration clause, who would make the best arbitrators to preside over the hearing, how much discovery must be conducted to prepare for the hearing, the level of formality necessary for the claim and client, and how soon the arbitration can be scheduled. Attorneys also need to prepare for how the arbitration will proceed from opening statements to summations, what exhibits and evidence are necessary to prove their case or defense, whether the lack of precedential value of the arbitrators' decision is a benefit or detriment, whether a confidential proceeding helps or hurts the client, and whether the arbitration should be binding or non-binding, to name just a few. There are advantages and disadvantages to arbitration and evaluating all of those for your clients and their individual situations will help you determine if it's a process that is best to resolve their dispute. However, when it's all said and done, an arbitration hearing closely resembles the different stages of a trial, from opening statements, direct and cross-examinations, exhibit presentations, to closing arguments. The biggest difference is the relaxed formality, because without a jury, there are fewer concerns that an arbitration panel will be prejudiced or swayed by the evidence presented as opposed to a jury.

Checkpoints

Although jurisdictional rules must always be consulted for the specifics of arbitration hearings in that area, most hearings follow the same format:

- Preliminary Matters—helps guide the parties through the discovery process, which is less strict than before trial, and work out the details of admitting evidence and witness testimony beforehand so that the hearing may run more smoothly.

- Opening Statements—each side's story of what their theme and theory of the case they will present. It familiarizes the arbitrators with what is to come during the hearing. The arbitrators may ask the attorneys questions during their opening statements about their case.

- Direct Examination—when an attorney conducts the questions of a witness for his side to highlight the testimony that will help his client's case.

- Cross-examination—when an attorney for the opponent questions the other side's witness to discredit the testimony or elicit testimony to help the opponent.

- Redirect Examination—when the attorney who conducted the witness's direct examination asks additional questions to repair any damage caused by the cross-examination.

- Objections—when attorneys want to request the arbitrators' ruling on keeping evidence from being admitted, requiring questions to be rephrased or stricken, or directing the witness to answer questions rather than be evasive.

- Exhibits and Evidence—documents, photos, testimony, or any other materials that either side needs to prove and support its claim or defense.

- Closing Statements/Summations—each side's chance to confirm that the testimony and evidence presented during the hearing supports their theme and theory of the case or defense, requiring that their side prevail. Again, the arbitrators may ask the attorneys questions during summation to clarify any ambiguities or concerns of the arbitrators.

Master Checklist

Negotiation — Communication and Emotion

- ❏ If there are emotional issues involved in a particular dispute, and you address them at the outset, your chances of reaching a resolution will be greatly increased.
- ❏ To communicate effectively, you need to think about what you are going to say and how it is going to be received. Venting or *lashing out* will get you nowhere because you are not communicating your true feelings.
- ❏ To communicate effectively, you need to *listen* to what is being said. Do not get defensive and try to formulate a response to justify your actions. Validate the message and the messenger.
- ❏ Even when the message is not clear, try to see through it and understand what the other side is trying to say.

Negotiation — Preparation

- ❏ You need to prepare thoroughly for a negotiation.
- ❏ Preparation includes identifying your interests *and* your opponent's interests. Don't stick to the surface. Dig deep.
- ❏ Once you have identified your interests and your opponent's interests, you have to look for solutions. Again, don't be satisfied with the obvious.
- ❏ Do a careful and objective analysis of your bargaining power. If you don't have any leverage, try to get some.

Negotiation — The Negotiation

- ❏ Patience is a virtue. It takes people a long time to change their mind.
- ❏ Be flexible. Things may not be as you see them. Be prepared to adjust.
- ❏ Be open. The other side might have some good ideas of their own.

❑ Feel the flow. Don't make an offer too quickly or too late. Don't be anxious to get to the end. Find the right time.

❑ Before you start negotiating, do your fact-finding. Ask questions. Get commitments if possible. Then you are ready to deal.

❑ Sell it, then tell it. Always give your reasons first. And make sure your reasons have a sound basis.

❑ Give yourself room to negotiate. Don't make an offer or demand you can't support with reasons, but make the best and highest offer or demand you can support. You can always come down, but you can't go up.

❑ Don't make a bad deal just to make a deal.

Mediation — Mediation and Mediators

❑ Judges prefer mediation to trial. Therefore in most jurisdictions, even where mediation is not mandatory, judges will refer you to mediation before setting the case for trial.

❑ If you voluntarily decide to go to mediation, you can control when to go and who the mediator will be.

❑ Lawyers can generally agree on a mediator.

❑ In mediation, the parties are much more involved in the outcome since they are the decision-makers.

❑ Mediators control the process of mediation.

❑ Mediators are usually trained and certified. In most jurisdictions, you don't have to be a lawyer to be a mediator.

❑ It's generally better to mediate with a certified mediator and a mediator experienced in the subject matter of the dispute.

Mediation — Timing

❑ The decision when to mediate depends on the facts and circumstances of each case.

Mediation — Process

❑ The mediator sets the tone for the mediation.

❑ The mediator in her opening statement will advise the parties that she is only a facilitator. She is not going to decide any legal issues. Her role is to assist the parties in reaching a settlement.

❏ The mediator will tell parties in her opening statement that everything said at mediation is confidential and that everything said in the private conferences is confidential.

❏ You, as the lawyer, control if your client is going to speak and how much your client is going to say at mediation.

❏ Normally, after the mediator's opening, both sides have the opportunity to give an opening statement.

❏ After opening statements, the mediator has the option of separating the parties or keeping them in joint session.

Mediation—Strategy

❏ You have to have a strategy in mediation that anticipates movement. You can make an offer and stick with it, but you are probably not going to reach a settlement.

❏ Make the highest offer you can support with reasons.

❏ After opening statements, the parties usually separate into separate rooms and the mediator takes over shuttling back and forth to discuss the pros and cons of each side's case in private session.

❏ A good mediator starts slow, taking time to get to know the parties, but eventually the mediator will be the tester of reality, making sure the parties don't alienate each other with bad offers and demands.

❏ It's the mediator's job to explore the parties' interests and try to formulate a settlement based on those interests.

❏ If the parties reach agreement, that agreement must be reduced to writing. While the mediation itself is confidential, the settlement agreement is not, unless the parties agree to keep it confidential.

Arbitration — The Mechanics of Arbitration: Commencement, Who and How Many Arbitrators

❏ The parties to a dispute need to know whether arbitration is mandatory (pursuant to contract, statute, or law) or voluntary. If mandatory, then the parties must resolve their dispute through arbitration; if voluntary, the parties can choose to resolve the dispute through arbitration.

❏ Once the parties decide arbitration is how their dispute is to be resolved, they must decide whether they will hire an administering agency or service to organize and supervise the proceedings, or whether they will conduct a non-administered/self-administered proceeding.

❏ Commencing the arbitration is the next step, which usually requires documents filed first by the claimant, describing the claims being brought against whom, and then by the respondent, responding to those claims and raising any counterclaims or defenses. Those documents are then usually served on the opposing party, with the court, and/or with the administering agency along with a filing fee.

❏ The parties must then decide whether one or three arbitrators will preside over the proceedings and how those arbitrators are chosen. The decision may be part of the parties' contract, decided by the administering agency, by law, or the parties' agreement.

❏ Usually arbitrators must be lawyers or law school graduates who have gone through some training and certification to be an arbitrator. Once certified, their names are placed on state-approved lists or within an administering agency's roster. If an arbitrator has expertise in a specialized area, that may be noted as well on these lists or rosters.

❏ If the parties have some say in who is an arbitrator, they should take an active role. They should carefully scrutinize arbitrators' backgrounds, experience, hiring history, etc. to help determine any biases they may have. Administering agencies will help vet the arbitrators' potential conflicts.

Arbitration — Rules, Time Frames, and Binding v. Non-Binding

❏ One benefit to resolving a dispute through arbitration is that you can schedule an arbitration hearing much sooner than a trial. Many administering agency rules require that an arbitration be resolved within so many days or months from commencement.

❏ If not governed by contract, rule, or statute, the parties may be able to decide whether they want the arbitration to be binding and therefore final as to the dispute, or non-binding and therefore more of an advisory opinion.

❏ Even if a non-binding decision is handed down by the arbitrators, the parties can agree to its terms and make it binding.

❏ Binding arbitration awards are final and may only be vacated or appealed or very limited grounds, such as an award being procured by a party's fraud or an arbitrator's corruption.

Arbitration—Discovery

❏ Arbitration discovery is intended to be simpler and less burdensome than litigation. Some administering agency rules and court rules limit the depth and scope of discovery to keep it more proportionate to the claims in dispute.

❏ The Federal Rules of Civil Procedure generally do not govern arbitrations specifically because it anticipates broader discovery designed for litigation. However, the purpose behind discovery—to level the playing field and ensure that each party has the documents and evidence to which it is entitled to support its claim or defense—does apply. Also, the rules requiring the parties act fairly and in good faith apply.

❏ The Federal Rules of Evidence generally do not apply to arbitrations, except for claims of privilege and work product.

❏ To increase the benefit of timeliness that arbitrations provide, some administering agency rules and parties have agreed to streamlined or expedited discovery to be completed within a shortened period of time.

❏ Arbitrators will generally hold preliminary conferences with parties to work out the details of discovery depth, scope, and deadlines. These conference may also address deadlines for motions, exchanging witness lists, etc.

❏ When additional discovery or evidentiary issues arise after the preliminary conference, additional conferences may be held, the disputes submitted to the arbitrators for resolution, or the arbitrators may make a decision on the spot.

Arbitration—Wrapping up the Mechanics of Arbitration

❏ Depending on the parties' contract, administering agency rules, or court rules, the arbitration hearing may be based on documents only with a supplemental hearing where the parties can appear by phone or virtually by computer. Otherwise, the hearing may be in person. However, if in person, the parties are usually encouraged to complete it within one to three days.

❏ The arbitrators' final award must be handed down in a timely manner once the hearing is completed. Usually, this must be within 7 to 30 days. The parties are then given a chance to point out any errors or corrections to be made to the award.

❏ Unless the parties agree otherwise, the award usually contains a brief explanation of the reasons behind the award.

❏ The arbitrators should designate whether the award is a "final" award for purposes of any related legal proceedings.

❏ The final award is a contract between the parties that must be followed or the non-breaching party may take action to have the contract enforced.

❏ Although the parties to an arbitration generally split the fees for the administering agency's service, arbitrators' rates, and room rental, arbitrators may apportion such fees differently as part of their award.

❏ Arbitrations are confidential proceedings and are therefore not open to the public.

❏ An award in one arbitration does not act as precedent in a later hearing. Each arbitration is decided on its own merits.

❏ There is no universal controlling law for arbitrations, and therefore the parties may agree to the law that will control, and if not, then the arbitrators may do so. However, arbitrators are generally not bound by legal precedent and can enter more creative awards to resolve the dispute than the law may allow. Additionally, arbitrators' awards may be less than a jury verdict because arbitrators are less swayed by emotion and heartfelt pleas.

Arbitration — The Hearing Under the Microscope

❏ Although jurisdictional rules must always be consulted for the specifics of arbitration hearings in that area, most hearings follow the same format:

❏ Preliminary Matters — helps guide the parties through the discovery process, which is less strict than before trial, and work out the details of admitting evidence and witness testimony beforehand so that the hearing may run more smoothly.

❏ Opening Statements — each side's story of what their theme and theory of the case they will present. It familiarizes the arbitrators with what is to come during the hearing. The arbitrators may ask the attorneys questions during their opening statements about their case.

❏ Direct Examination — when an attorney conducts the questions of a witness for his side to highlight the testimony that will help his client's case.

❏ Cross-Examination — when an attorney for the opponent questions the other side's witness to discredit the testimony or elicit testimony to help the opponent.

❏ Redirect Examination — when the attorney who conducted the witness's direct examination asks additional questions to repair any damage caused by the cross-examination.

❏ Objections — when attorneys want to request the arbitrators' ruling on keeping evidence from being admitted, requiring questions to be rephrased or stricken, or directing the witness to answer questions rather than be evasive.

❏ Exhibits and Evidence — documents, photos, testimony, or any other materials that either side needs to prove and support its claim or defense.

❏ Closing Statements/Summations — each side's chance to confirm that the testimony and evidence presented during the hearing supports their theme and theory of the case or defense, requiring that their side prevail. Again, the arbitrators may ask the attorneys questions during summation to clarify any ambiguities or concerns of the arbitrators.

Index